Finding Clarity

Design a Business You Love and Simplify Your Marketing

By Amanda H. Young

Copyright

Cover Design: John Matthews
Editing: Grace Kerina

Advance Praise

"*Finding Clarity* is honest, enjoyable, and fresh in content and style. As a business owner for well over a decade myself, I have often had to stop and ask myself, 'Why am I doing this?' Amanda helps us to ask ourselves all the right questions, get to the heart of the matter, and uncover the answers needed to be successful business owners and entrepreneurs. I strongly recommend this book for the business owner who needs to build a business, revamp the business, or get a booster shot to remember the whys. *Why am I doing this?* Because Amanda Young's book facilitates the process so that I can remind myself that this is my passion and that I do what I love and love what I do! Thank you, Amanda!"

– Hilary Cummings, M.Ed., Founder and Executive Director, Education Outside the Box, www.eotb.org

"If you're just starting a business or need more clients, read this book. More importantly – do the exercises in the book! Most entrepreneurs think they know the answers, but they often don't sit down to work out the details. That's where Amanda's step-by-step process really helps. This book is loaded with exercises you can do to shift how you think about your business and your clients. If you're tired of fluff books, this is the book for you. Look inside. Get Clarity."

– Leah Jackman-Wheitner, PhD, www.leahjackman.com

"I worked 'around' my business for several years without really working 'on' it. Mainly because I didn't really know what to do. There are so many resources out there that tell you how you can build a great business, just like some other person did. But Young turns that advice on its head and tells you how to find your business by ALLOWING it to come from you. This book helped me think about how to build a thriving, unique business by really understanding who I am and what I have to offer. She helped to clarify and distill those thoughts and feelings that have been in the back of my mind and deep in my soul telling me THIS is how I'm meant to help people on my road to becoming a successful entrepreneur."
– *Sharee Calverley Lawler*

"If you are going to read one book this year to help you gain clarity around your business (or business idea) THIS is the book. *Finding Clarity* helps you do just that – find clarity!

I didn't know what to expect when I opened the book, but Amanda writes with clarity (imagine that!) and humor and I was immediately drawn into the pages of her book. I found myself relating to her experiences. I, too, had hired several coaches, yet I was still 'Cloudy with a Chance of Meatballs,' meaning I was trying different things to see what 'stuck.' I realized I was not alone. Others had experienced the same fuzziness and frustration.

Amanda so effortlessly and quickly cut through the fog. I plan to recommend this book to all of my friends, because, as Amanda said in her book, I also want to 'find a better way to serve my clients' so they don't have to go through what I did.

Thank you, Amanda, for your clarity and humor in this book and for helping me to find clarity in my work. I feel a renewed sense of excitement!"
– Ann Magee, www.YourSoulLife.com

"Finally! The help I've been waiting for! Who would have thought you could blend intuition and marketing? Amanda did! I love the way she offers suggestions to use your intuition to design a successful business that you love. Using her suggestions and answering her questions based on what *I* want and need makes my business feel very personal and even closer to my heart than before. Amanda helped me get clear on what I really want so that I've fallen in love with my business and can give it the attention it needs to thrive. Thank you, Amanda!"
– Jennifer Blumenthal, CCC, Soul Mentor, Intuitive, Healer, Coach, www.JenniferBlumenthal.com

"Being an entrepreneur is one of the busiest professions out there, but you can choose to be overwhelmed by your busyness or find sanity in your business by following Amanda's step-by-step guide in the Process of ALLOWING Clarity. I choose *Finding Clarity*. You should too."
– Pamela Mattei, President and Founder, DyeSigns By Pamela, Inc. www.dyesignsbypamelainc.com

"*Finding Clarity* cuts through all the clutter and noise surrounding entrepreneurs, lets them release the pressure around what they think they should be doing, and helps them identify the key actions they need to be doing to be successful.

Finding Clarity is a wonderfully honest and insightful guide to creating the business that you love. Starting and growing a business can feel overwhelming. Amanda Young's insight will help you avoid the Seductive Shoulds and other pitfalls. Learn how to build a business that is satisfying and successful on your own terms.

As a Confidence Coach for women, I'll be recommending this to my clients who are looking for clarity in their own businesses."
– Denise Fountain, Confident Moms Confident Kids Coaching, www.denisefountain.com

"Reading this book was a very productive use of my afternoon! I came away with many actionable insights, but what resonated most with me was the discussion on inward-facing vs. outward-facing businesses. Instead of doing what you think others want you to do, your business success comes from doing what you want to do for people you love. I've made many notes and am looking forward to putting this into action."
– Sara Mersinger

"*Finding Clarity* is the book for entrepreneurs tired of hearing that they need to constantly be "hustling." Instead, Young offers a different approach. One that encourages the reader to tap into who she really is and

build her business from there, because no amount of 'hustling' can replace YOU in your business."
– *Evie Burke, One Insight Closer, Inc. www.oneinsightcloser.com*

"I have always been roadblocked at the concept of finding referral partners. The chapter 'Inspire Referrals' in Amanda Young's book *Finding Clarity* made me feel like I finally get it and will be able to connect with referral partners in an authentic way. It was her easy-to-understand concepts of 'redefining networking' and finding your 'power partners' that made me feel like I will finally be able to network and find referral partners in a way that feels congruent with my personality."
– *Lissa Sandler, Web Presence Academy, www.webpresenceacademy.com*

"Amazing! I read this book a week ago and asked myself, 'Why not try these easy steps in my business?' I started to follow Amanda's advice the next day, step-by-step. In one week I got amazing results! Just one week and everything changed."

I read *Finding Clarity* much more carefully a second time and decided to write a review. Please, spend a few hours and this book will change your business for the better."
– *Alexander Molodin, Ph.D., Owner and Head Manager of a design company*

Dedication

To Rick, for supporting, encouraging, and holding space
for me to find clarity.

Table of Contents

Introduction

In business, as in most things we do in life, we need to know where we want to go to have any chance of getting there. If we know we want to get away from home for a bit to relax and unwind on a vacation, it will serve us well to define what it means to us to get away from home and how we prefer to unwind. Two weeks with your in-laws might get you out of the house but not be what you would consider relaxing. Taking a sightseeing tour of Europe when you really want a beach vacation in the Caribbean is unlikely to produce the results you desire.

Often, entrepreneurs struggle with the issue of not knowing what they want in their business. We aren't sure who we want to serve, or we think we should serve "anyone with a pulse." We aren't sure what to offer, so we offer a little bit of everything. And we sure don't know how to create businesses we love, because we think work must be hard if we want to see any real results. We're overwhelmed by all the options to promote, build, and expand our business. We want to cast a wide net with our messaging and have the biggest target market in hopes of catching as many clients as possible. And we think that by being vague we're leaving our options open so that we never miss a great opportunity.

The general business advice we received growing up came from a place of scarcity and fear left over from past generations of people who had survived the Depression and lived when times were tough. Their message was clear: "Take what you can get." Sadly, many entrepreneurs are stuck in that old world, struggling to unleash their true talents in ways that will be of service to their clients. We work with clients we don't love and take jobs we aren't good at because we need to pay the bills, living by the idea that "a bad paying client is better than no client at all."

All this confusion and lack of clarity around what we truly want and where we want to go in our business provides the perfect environment for stress, overwhelm, and decision paralysis that prevents us from taking meaningful action toward our goals. The random and conflicting advice we've received from myriad sources is left swirling around in our heads, leading us to think we should be doing *more*. More of what, we aren't exactly sure, but more of it. Surely, doing more networking, social media, online advertising, blogging, webinars, teleconferences, workshops, flyers, and posters will magically save our businesses by driving massive numbers of customers our way and thus solving all our problems.

Add to all that the feeling that we're so busy we can't take the time to constructively think about or work on our business, we keep moving along in the same groove, hoping our momentum will magically guide us to the promised land of business success. That mindless movement is an illusion because we are only swimming in circles and exhausting ourselves in the deep end of the pool, instead of swimming with a purpose to the shallow depths to take a breather.

Worst of all, we end up beating ourselves up for not being able to figure all of this out on our own. We know it's not rocket science. It can't be *that* hard, and yet we can't seem to get the pieces to fit together in a way that makes sense. Just like we can't see our nose because it's on our face, we're too close to our businesses. We know we're good at some things and we know we can help people, but we aren't quite sure how it all comes together. Unless someone else is reflecting it to us like a mirror – we can't see it. And that frustrates us to no end because we're smart. We should be able to figure this out on our own. We should be able to run a successful business that helps people and makes good money, right?

We've invested a significant amount of money into hiring vendors to design our websites and hiring business coaches who helped a little here or there. We've tapped into the support of friends who offered advice or listened but who weren't experts in our field, and maybe did more harm than good. We've tried to rely on our spouses, who end up feeling bad for not being able to fix our business problems.

Remind me – why do we do all of this? Oh, right. It's because we want a successful business helping others while making enough money to live the good life: taking relaxing European vacations with our families, remodeling our homes so we can host parties and create memories with our friends, driving luxury cars that make errands more fun, and giving generously to charities we believe in – while also building that cushy nest egg so it'll be waiting for us when we reach retirement age.

Although, as entrepreneurs, we're starting to suspect, we'll likely never retire.

20/20 Vision

Imagine what the world would be like if we knew where we wanted to go with our business. Imagine if we knew what we were good at, who we wanted to help, what we wanted to do for them, and how to design our businesses to support *our* needs as we help the people we most want to help, instead of doing what everyone else thinks we *should* be doing. What if we listened to our guts and allowed ourselves to be led by our intuition instead of our need to pay the bills each month? Instead of chasing clients, spending countless resources hunting them down, and convincing them we have the solutions they need, our best clients would be attracted by our clear messaging and would effortlessly ask to work with us. Instead of being stressed out and overwhelmed by all the options of where our business could go, what would it be like to make decisions confidently and take deliberate actions toward achieving our goals?

We would be doing what we love, for people we love to work with, on our terms, while making the impact and income we desire and deserve. We would schedule time to work on our business, plan where we're going, and proceed with focused confidence that eludes most entrepreneurs yet is a proven catalyst for success. We would be present and available for our families and friends, enjoy luxurious vacations, and create breathing room for our minds that would allow us to embrace the present moment. Our dreams would find us. And we would allow the whole process to be easy, simple, and fun.

If the prospect of designing a business to support your own needs as you share your innate gifts scares you, that's a sign you're on the right path. That's your ego trying to protect you. As an entrepreneur, you're a bit of a rebel. It's normal for rebels like us to take chances and extend beyond our comfort zones. That's where true growth happens.

You might worry that you can't possibly make money doing what you're good at for clients you enjoy serving. But think of all the actors, musicians, and inventors who win awards for sharing their amazing talents with the world and doing what they love. You might buy into the idea that following your passion won't pay the bills. The truth is the opposite. When you're led by your passion, money flows freely. You might think you need another certification or degree to be a true expert in your field. But you only need to be a few steps ahead of the people you serve to guide them successfully along the path you've already taken. You might believe that it will take too long, cost too much, or be too difficult, but with the right mixture of sound advice that helps you find the clarity you need to design a business you love, and with focused action steps to move toward your goals, you really can create the success of your dreams.

ALLOWING Clarity

In this book, I'll guide you through the three stages of my unique, eight-step Process of ALLOWING Clarity, designed to guide you in creating your business and taking deliberate actions toward your goals (instead of using the spaghetti method of throwing what you've got against the wall and hoping something sticks).

The eight steps of the Process of ALLOWING Clarity are divided into three stages: Design Selfishly, Communicate Clearly and Act Imperfectly. We'll cover each of the steps in detail, and for each step I'll share success stories, lessons learned, and simple questions you can ask yourself. The result is clarity around your business and what you want, the ability to talk about what you do in a meaningful way, and a straight cut through the clutter so you can take the right actions to support your success.

Chapter 1 – Confusion and Uncertainty

When I started my business as a solopreneur, marketing strategist, business coach, and consultant, I hobbled along, as clueless as ever. It didn't matter that I was highly educated and had followed all of society's unwritten rules to become successful. I'd done well in school, gone to a good college, gotten a degree in business, had a few jobs in advertising, gotten married, gone back to school for an advanced degree, bought a home, had children, and... found myself wildly unfulfilled in my career and struggled to define myself. I didn't know what I wanted. I only knew I hated working for egotistical bosses who couldn't harness my potential, didn't allow me to do my best work, and didn't see the vision I saw of what amazing things could be created in this world and their companies.

After graduate school, my husband and I moved to Chicago for his career and I decided to become a "consultant," because that was a title with prestige and consultants made good money, even though no one seemed to understand what they did. I thought being a consultant would give me the flexibility I needed to take whatever work came my way and allow me to pay the bills. But I had no idea what I was doing. I didn't know who might hire me, what I should charge them, or how to find them. I'd read dozens of books on finding my purpose, starting a business, becoming an entrepreneur. I'd read countless issues of *Inc. Magazine* and *Entrepreneur* from cover to cover. And I *still* didn't know what to do. I continued to struggle while my friends got "real" jobs with "real" salaries and "real" opportunities for career growth. I was terrified, lost in uncharted territory, and felt alone trying to figure it all out by myself.

It didn't seem to matter that I had taken courses on entrepreneurship in undergrad, interned with an entrepreneurial company in graduate school, or attended workshops at the Women's Business Development Center to learn how to launch my small business the "right" way. Informational interviews with professionals in a handful of service industries helped build my network but didn't help me get any clearer about how I could start my own business or put my vast marketing education and years of job experience to work.

After limping along for years, I stumbled across a business coach who had a system to help me launch my business. She had a track record for success, a community of like-minded entrepreneurs who I could work with through her process, and she held my hand in a way that made launching my business a little more manageable and less lonely. It was everything I dreamed of… until the moment when she said, "Now it's time to get really clear about your business. If you don't know what you want to do or who you want to work with, just imagine that you do know and make something up." That one piece of advice broke me. She was pretty much saying, "Build your business based on a fictitious guess and see what happens. You can tweak and tune it later."

To me, that meant, "Don't worry. You can build your house on this crappy foundation, and we'll move it later. It doesn't have to be a good house. It just has to look sort of like a house that someone might want someday." My insides were screaming, "Do you have any idea how hard it will be to fix this later?"

At the same time, I was distracted by my bank balance, which was badly in need of a boost, to the point where any chance I had of inviting clarity to shine into my world and illuminate the idea of what I wanted my business to be was being choked off with each passing day of increasing stress.

Since I couldn't think of a better option, I did what the coach had said to do. One week, my business focus, my "house," was a flimsy tent on the beach in the form of a marketing company targeting small business owners in the local community who didn't know how to find clients. The next week, it was a drafty shack in the woods where I thought I wanted to publish books on motherhood and become a serious mom blogger. Each week I had a new idea and reinvented my business, all the while seething inside and wishing for someone to sit me down and help me work it all out. I knew I loved writing, marketing, and helping entrepreneurs, but I wasn't sure how I could string all of that together to make something beautiful. I needed someone to help me filter through all the chatter in my head so I could come up with a scalable plan for creating a successful business that got me to my goals while allowing me the freedom to be present for the adorable daughter and handsome son I was determined to spend more time with than any nanny or daycare ever would.

Seeking Answers Elsewhere

I tried investing in a small group program to set the stage for launching my business. When that wasn't enough, I signed up for a full year of coaching around learning how to market my business, even though I didn't know what my business was beyond a vague concept of helping entrepreneurs, or maybe nonprofits, with their marketing.

When I scored my first big client, I was sure that was a sign from the universe that I was meant to help nonprofit law schools dying from low enrollment. Instead, I learned that they were not the best client for me to serve. I wanted clients who would take more action on the ideas we conceived together, instead of paying someone (me) to blame when things didn't work out how they'd hoped.

When that year of coaching around marketing was up, I realized I'd learned a lot, but I *still* felt fuzzy about my business, how to talk about it, who I was meant to work with, and how I was going to find them. I didn't feel like my business fit into the formula suggested by my coach. I probably could have made it work, but something about it didn't feel right. Something was missing. I craved individual attention, one-on-one support to help me apply what I had learned to my unique situation in a way that highlighted my strengths and talents. I didn't want to conform to a set, pre-defined program. I wanted someone who had a buffet of options to help me load my plate with a balanced meal that would fuel my soul.

My next coach was a life coach. She helped me clear out the mental clutter that was holding me back from success and taught me to trust myself and my intuition. As I followed her guidance, my emotions evened out, my power shifted, and business improved from the previous year. I was on track to hit my goal of $100,000 for the year – double my previous year – so I wasn't feeling like a complete failure, but I was hiding in the security of big clients who paid well but didn't do the work they needed to do to get the results they supposedly wanted. All my eggs were in a handful of baskets that couldn't easily be replenished if any of them went away. That didn't feel right. I was still spinning my wheels, chasing my tail, and swimming in circles with a lot of half-baked ideas and concepts, but there was nothing concrete I could point to that was the problem.

To serve more clients and help them achieve better results, I invested in yet another coach who specifically trained entrepreneurs how to create online courses and design businesses that led their clients through a signature process. I invested in software and flew to another retreat to get more personal attention in a small group setting. I learned a lot. I made more connections. I even got a client referral from the program. But I still had more questions than answers, more debt than income, and more confusion than clarity.

Internal Clarity and Confidence

Finally, I hired a more rebellious coach, one who taught me how to throw out all the rules and approach my business from a different perspective altogether. Instead of listening to what everyone else thought I should do, I needed to listen to what *I* wanted to do. Instead of identifying a traditional target market, I needed to conceptualize *one person* I wanted to work with. Instead of identifying a specific niche market, I needed to focus on the common *outcomes* my clients wanted and were actually getting. Instead of creating a beautiful website and fancy logo, I needed to put out offers targeting that person I'd conceptualized who I wanted to help – and keep doing that until I hit on an offer that resonated with my clients.

It wasn't fair for me to compare myself to the super successful rock stars who had been in the marketplace for years and to pressure myself into magically achieving their same results overnight. Taylor Swift didn't start out performing in sold-out stadiums. Oprah Winfrey didn't start out with her own television studio. Julia Roberts didn't land a leading film role straight out of acting school. While success can come overnight for some, it can also grow organically as your goals become clear. With clarity comes confidence. With confidence comes success.

The point is, if I had an idea that I believed in and felt was worthwhile, I shouldn't give up on it after one quick try. That would be letting my ego win by proving my failure and keeping me restricted to my zone of safety, where I wouldn't be exposed to any of the scary evils success might bring.

The key was having a coach who had experience with helping others like me succeed, who knew how to draw out her clients' visions for what they wanted, and who could help me translate that vision into action steps that were achievable in a way that produced fast results with low upfront investment. This was what I'd needed – someone who could reflect my inner wisdom to me in a way I was able to understand; someone who nudged me forward when things got uncomfortable and gave me the courage to continue by holding the vision of my success when I lost sight of it. With her help, I was able to harness the power of my vision and take action one step at a time toward achieving my goals.

Fast Forward

All told, I invested over $20,000 in coaching in less than three years while bringing in a total income of just over $100,000. I was so determined to crack the code and find a better way to serve my clients so that they didn't have to suffer the same way I did. I wanted to create a system to help entrepreneurs do what I'd finally done: fast forward through the stress, financial hardship, and time spent trying to make a bad situation with crummy client work, just so they could pay the bills. I wanted to facilitate clarity early on in the process of growing a business, so that if it needed to shift at a future date, that didn't mean dismantling a drafty shack in the woods but putting a key in the ignition and driving a motor home across town with little cost or effort.

Follow Your Own Path

Using the Process of ALLOWING Clarity, I've helped entrepreneurs work through being stuck in overwhelm to the point of not being able to serve their clients, paralyzed by what they thought they should be doing and what they assumed their business needed to be. By helping clients answer basic questions about what they *really* wanted and what their vision was for the success of their company, they uncovered insights that released all the pressure they'd built up and imagined around what they *should* be doing or how they thought business *should* be done. Then they were free to focus on what worked best for them and their individual needs. If there's one thing I've learned, it's that entrepreneurship isn't one-size-fits-all.

In working with Heather, a client with a successful business as a personal stylist for business professionals, the Process of ALLOWING Clarity helped her gain confidence in her marketing, clarity around her business goals, and identify the actions that would help her realize those goals, while also quieting the mind chatter that was holding her back.

The Process of ALLOWING Clarity showed Heather that she didn't want to expand her business to have multiple employees, but she did want an assistant to handle her administrative tasks so that she could spend more time shopping with her clients and building their style confidence. We quickly realized that she was beating herself up for not being better about writing blog entries and posting on social media, tasks she'd heard everyone talking about. She thought that by not doing more social media and blogging she was missing out on great clients. But social media wasn't the source of her true client base. While it could get her leads and referrals, she was better off presenting to area law firms and providing shopping and styling services so that lawyers felt comfortable in their choice of clothing and exuded confidence in the courtroom.

By getting the clarity she needed, Heather was able to avoid investing time and money on social media strategies she hated doing. Instead, she got to take action and focus on doing what she loved with the right clients.

Sponge or Source

Throughout this process, you can spend time gathering from others all the information you could ever need about what you should do, who you should serve, or how you should run your business. You can be a sponge absorbing everyone else's ideas and trying to configure them into some semblance of a plan. Or you can be the source for the ideas and actions that make your business successful. You can choose to design your business selfishly, in a way that supports your needs, your talents, and your favorite customers. This is the power the Process of ALLOWING Clarity will give you – the power that comes from being truly yourself.

Chapter 2 – The Process of ALLOWING Clarity

In this short chapter, I'll give you an overview of the Process of ALLOWING Clarity, the system that helps my clients move forward in their businesses. Its three stages, which each consist of a few steps, are designed to help entrepreneurs find the answers they need so they can take deliberate action. This can be a big and relieving switch from wasting precious time, money, and resources on trying anything and everything to see what sticks.

The Process of ALLOWING Clarity starts with being more selfish in your business. Instead of doing what others think you should be doing, or what others say your clients need, or what you hope will make the most money, you need to Design Selfishly – that's the first stage of the ALLOWING process.

Once you've designed your business in a way that supports your needs and considers your unique gifts and talents, move to the second stage, where you'll focus on how to Communicate Clearly. Many entrepreneurs don't know how to talk about their businesses in a way that attracts clients. They're so busy being in their business that they don't always know how to talk about the services they provide and the results they can achieve for their clients. Clarifying your communications will go a long way toward connecting you with the people you most want to help.

Stage 3 of the ALLOWING process – Act Imperfectly – is where it all comes together. Perfection and the need to have a polished image all too often paralyzes entrepreneurs and keeps them from their success. Needing to have everything in place before you can serve your clients simply isn't necessary. Making mistakes and learning from them is one of the main reasons for becoming an entrepreneur in the first place. Your mistakes, as painful as they may seem in the moment, provide some of the best opportunities for growth. They're where the real learning takes place that helps you hone your offerings and step into the success that's tailor-made for you.

The three stages in the Process of ALLOWING Clarity are composed of the following eight steps:

Stage 1 – Design Selfishly

A – All about you. Get clear on who you are and what unique gifts you have to share with the world so that you can use them to your advantage in your business.

L – Listen to your heart. Use your intuition to design your business to support your needs and unique abilities, and understand your reason for being in business, instead of trying to meet someone else's expectations, so that you can love what you do.

L - Love your clients. Clearly understand who it is you serve, what they want, need, fear, desire, and where to find them, so that you know when the perfect client is knocking at your door and when you need to let go of clients who aren't a match for your services.

O - Offer to lead. Match your skills with what clients need, so that you can be of service to them in the best possible way while leading them on a clear path to the solution you provide. Describe the problem you solve, the opportunity you present, and the outcome your clients want in a way that they can understand and that attracts who you want it to attract.

Stage 2 – Communicate Clearly

W - Write your pitch. Know what to say when someone asks what you do. Create a simple message that clearly communicates what you do, who you serve, and the results you get for your clients so that you can talk about your business in a way that piques interest and sparks conversation.

I - Inspire referrals. Understand how to find the right style of networking to find and attract your favorite clients, while also attending the right networking opportunities and seeking out your ideal referral partners.

Stage 3 – Act Imperfectly

N- Notice your needs. Get the support you need to work smarter, faster, and with more resources and knowledge at your disposal, so you can reach your goals more quickly and with less stress.

G - Go! Take action! Cut through the clutter of busywork to identify which opportunities will pay off and support your goals, and which actions are a waste of your time and investment, so that you can streamline your path to success.

* * *

The Process of ALLOWING Clarity prompts you to ponder questions you may not have considered before launching your business. These questions and explorations are designed to guide you to thoughtful, meaningful insights that save time, money, and heartache as you're struggling to define an existing business.

I hope you allow the answers to come from a place deep inside you – the place that holds the wisdom of your true self. Allowing your inner wisdom to shine is the key to finding clarity. With a clear idea of what's right for you and your business, you can take the right actions to achieve the success of your dreams.

Stage 1 – Design Selfishly

"My will is mine... I shall not make it soft for you."
Aeschylus, *Agamemnon*

The first four steps of the Process of ALLOWING Clarity focus on you and your truth and voice.

Our goal as entrepreneurs is to be successful. After all, we don't embark on this journey to create a failed empire. From the very beginning, as with most of life's endeavors, you receive advice in every shape, size, and form along the way. Wisdom will come from experts who have walked the path before you and speak their truth from their experiences. Insights will arise from less qualified, but equally opinionated, influencers who urge you to change course.

The key to becoming a successful entrepreneur is knowing which pieces of advice to keep and how to resist and release the rest. The only voice that truly matters as an entrepreneur is your voice.

By designing your business selfishly, you'll avoid the temptation to take detours off your chosen path and wander around without fulfilling your true purpose. When you allow yourself to trust your intuition, listen to your heart, and lead your business in a way that is true to yourself, you'll build your business on a solid foundation of confidence and clarity.

Chapter 3 – All About You

"My life didn't please me, so I created my life."
Coco Chanel

*A*LLOWING – *A* is for *A*ll About You

When navigating uncharted territory, as most entrepreneurs do, it's best to start out heading in the direction of what you know. Then you can build your skills and knowledge along the way while gaining insight into what you still need to learn to arrive at your destination.

The first step in the Process of ALLOWING Clarity is to get to know All About You. That doesn't mean you need to know everything about yourself right now. We're looking for a snapshot of who you truly are at this point in time. If you loved dogs as a child, now prefer cats, and someday hope to own a farm with horses, the cats are where you are now. It means that all your focus needs to be on your skills, your talents, your abilities, your knowledge, your preferences, and your current view of the world. No one else's opinions, suggestions, or needs matter during this step in the ALLOWING process.

Connect with Your Inner Voice

You can choose to figure out who you are like I did –
by outwardly surveying everyone I knew to see who they
thought I was and what I should do. Or you can skip that
painful, time-consuming step and allow your inner voice
to show you who you really are. That doesn't mean you
have to do this alone or that no one can help you along
the way. It means that you'll be presented with a lot of
different options. Your inner voice needs to be the
loudest. Many of you might not be able to hear that inner
voice very well just yet, so I'll offer some tips for
amplifying your inner voice along the way. Your inner
voice will help you easily filter your options into two
categories: true you and not you.

You're doing this process because, once you know
your true self, you can shine your inner light more
brightly than ever before. Your passion for what you do
will light up the sky, similar to how Commissioner
Gordon illuminated the clouds with a spotlight and the
bat symbol to get Batman's attention when Gotham City
needed rescuing. Your clarity around who you are will
magnetically attract the clients you are meant to work
with, serve, and help – while repelling those who aren't a
match for your talents.

Finding your passion and inner light can be the tough
part. While I know we all have unique talents that we've
been put here to share, uncovering them can be tricky.
For some people, discovering their unique gifts comes
naturally. Just like their heart beats or air fills and
escapes their lungs with each passing breath, they know
their purpose. Take my husband as an example. It's no

secret at my house that I have always envied how he clearly knew he wanted to be an Architect from an early age. Meanwhile, I meandered from job to job trying to string together a career that mixed helping people with marketing with being my own boss. He clearly wanted to work for a leading design firm in a big city to help create buildings that supported their users. I fuzzily wanted help putting all my knowledge and book-smarts to use to help more people with their service businesses. His career fit into a neat little box. Mine was a hot mess that resembled a knotted ball of yarn after having been batted around by a handful of kittens on catnip.

Somewhere along the way, I bought into the story that getting clear about what I wanted wasn't allowed, being selfish was always bad, and finding my passion was going to be hard. I unknowingly buried my light, did what I thought others wanted, and made it hard to find my true answers. I answered every question with, "I don't know." Or, worse, I copied someone else's answers so that I didn't have to find my own.

No matter the path you take to get to clarity around your purpose or passion or inner light, the critical part of this process is to be true to yourself. It's *all about you*. Allow your inner voice to rise and calm your mind long enough to see, feel, or hear it when it does.

Shakespeare says it best in Hamlet as Polonius explains:

"This above all: to thine own self be true, / And it must follow, as the night the day, / Thou canst not then be false to any man."

The Hard Way

A friend of mine, back when I lived in Milwaukee and was learning how to knit with an eclectic group of talented women, pulled me aside before we headed into our knitting club on a beautiful fall evening on the shores of Lake Michigan. I could see that she was upset as she confessed she had just been let go from her big agency job in public relations. Tears were welling up in her eyes and ready to escape her lower lid. It was early in her career, she was truly passionate and dedicated to her work, and it was the first time she had ever been fired.

I looked at her and blurted out, "Congratulations! That's great news!"

In shock, she shook her head and her eyes got wide with confusion.

I continued. "Just last week you were complaining about how much you hated going to work, how it wasn't a good fit, and how you weren't happy there. I know it sucks to be fired and feels awful to not have a job, but if you take a second to spin around to my side of this situation, you'll see that this is wonderful!"

She started to chuckle and a smile spread across her face.

"Think about it," I said. "Now you can collect unemployment – that's why you pay into it – and you can focus all of your efforts on finding a job that is a better fit for you and your talents. This really is great news."

Right then and there, something shifted inside her and, while she wasn't quite ready to shut down her pity party completely, she started to think of how losing her job could be an opportunity and spent the rest of the night bouncing from mourning the loss of her job to imagining what was yet to come. She took the feedback she got from her former boss and used it to learn more about what she wanted in her career and, ultimately, she understood why she was better off having been let go. It was an opportunity to get closer to what she wanted in a fulfilling career.

We often learn a lot more when things don't work out than we learn when they do.

Reflection question: Think of a time when you learned a great life lesson when something didn't work out as planned. What happened?

The Easy Way

One thing I know for sure is, if you are reading this book, you're a natural-born leader. You might not always be in charge or want to be responsible for how things turn out, but as an entrepreneur, you must lead to succeed.

Part of being a good leader is knowing your strengths and *making decisions that support those strengths*. After all, do you want your bookkeeper cutting your hair? You don't go to a podiatrist for help with a broken wrist. And if you love being an amazing pet photographer, you should decide not to photograph skyscrapers, because that isn't what you're best at or what you love doing.

For some of you, knowing who you are and what makes you unique comes easily. For others, it may take more time, more quiet space, or more help. If you are struggling to see your true strengths, or want to confirm your suspicions, I'll explain a few different ways you can uncover them. As you conduct your search, I encourage you to watch for themes across the answers you receive. Don't ever check this task off your to-do list, as it will never be complete.

These insights are priceless when it comes to honing your business and your focus. Always be on the lookout for ways to increase your awareness of your strengths and incorporate them into your business.

Relax and Have Fun

Before we get started down this path, I invite you to take a deep breath. Maybe shake your arms, wiggle your body, or dance to your favorite song. Some people find seated meditation helps to clear their minds, I find that cleaning my kitchen and sweeping my floors works better. It doesn't matter how you destress as much as it matters that you relax into the process. I want you to loosen up and have fun because that's how to get the best results. If you are worried, tense, stressed out, and fearful that you'll select the wrong answer, make the wrong choice, or go down the wrong path, you will. The pressure you put yourself under to get this "right" is the very reason you are reading this book. For fast-moving, go-getting, doers like us, it isn't always easy to let go and relax.

If it helps, create a list of all the worries you have around this process of getting clear in your business and either put them into an imaginary cauldron or place them in a physical box with a lid so that they are in a temporary holding space while you free up the rest of your mind to have some fun.

The Outer Way – Unveil Your True Strengths

Take a deep breath and read the practical suggestions below to see which ones appeal to you for starting to learn all about you and home in on your true strengths.

Ask five people who know you well to honestly list your top five personality traits. When I did this, it revealed my natural ability to talk to strangers with ease. That one observation, noted by multiple friends, led me to understand that I'm a natural networker and connector. While that's something that comes incredibly easy to me, it is something many people struggle with whenever they meet someone new.

List five topics you could talk about for hours or write a book about. Is there a topic that your friends are sick of hearing from you about? Or do you get repeat questions on the same topic that you could answer in your sleep? They don't have to relate to your education, upbringing, or previous career path. You might have a degree in art history and realize that you could talk for hours about how to train a new puppy. Remember to throw out all the preconceived ideas you have about what you think you should be doing. Allow space for all your talents to surface.

Take a personality test. Chances are you've already taken some sort of personality test that helped you identify some of your strongest characteristics and traits. The challenge with this option is finding a test that clicks for you. There are a lot of tests available. Some are free and others charge a nominal fee. But the results can cover a wide variety of aspects about yourself. Similar to how the sorting hat in Harry Potter placed each Hogwarts student into the house that best fits their personality, my results from the Myers-Briggs Type Indicator (www.myersbriggs.org) sorted me as an INFJ – Introversion (I), iNtuition (N), Feeling (F), and Judgment (J). The INFJ label explains why I like working from home and expend energy in social settings, focus on the big picture and the future, use less logic and more personal connections to make decisions, and love to plan and be on time.

One personality test wasn't enough for me, as I needed to be sure I had exactly the right answer, and I wasn't hearing much from my gut – which means I didn't trust myself to know what was best for me so I wasn't listening to my intuition. I took the Gallup StrengthsFinder to identify my top strengths and found my personality type using the Enneagram. The Gallup StrengthsFinder (www.gallupstrengthscenter.com) was amazingly insightful and helped me see just how strong and rare my strategic thinking skills were. Learning how unique your combination of strengths is (mine was one in 33 Million) using that assessment is truly eye-opening and confidence-boosting. I accredit that to having more concrete, third-party confirmation of your abilities.

The Enneagram (www.enneagraminstitute.com) wasn't as clear for me at first since my results were inconsistent. I finally settled into the idea that I was what the Enneagram classified as a "Seven" or "The Enthusiast" despite considering myself an introvert.

Later on in the ALLOWING process, we'll use the insights you gain around introversion and extroversion to make your networking more effective.

The key to all these assessments is to watch for characteristics that combine to form themes. If you're great at talking to strangers, hosting parties with a wide range of guests, and encouraging friendships, that all adds up to being a great community builder.

Reflection question: Which characteristics can combine into themes that will reveal your true talents?

Pay attention to compliments you receive. Think about a time when someone said, "I can't believe you did that and made it look so easy!" and you responded, "That's just what I do." It's the subtle talents you have that are often revealed to be your hidden superpowers. When you hear compliments repeated, instead of brushing them off and thinking someone is just trying to flatter you, stop to allow them to soak in. Take a moment to think about their comment and what it really means about you and your gifts.

When we bought a new home, I hosted a housewarming party two months after moving in. My neighbors kept saying, "You're amazing! I could never have gotten settled that quickly let alone invited the entire block over for a party!" At first, I shrugged these comments off and went about my day. It wasn't until I sat and thought about them that I realized I'm great at pulling parties together, gathering mixed groups of friends, and not worrying about if my house is in show-ready condition.

When another compliment surfaced at a coaching retreat, I was much more aware that it was unveiling another one of my superpowers. A friend approached to congratulate me on building such an amazing community within our coaching group. It was something that I did so naturally I didn't notice that everyone else couldn't do it. I like to think of it as being a strong swimmer and not realizing how good you are until you win a race by the length of the pool.

Work with a coach who can act as a mirror and reflect your talents to you in a way that feels right. While all the methods I have listed previously will help you gain clarity around your unique strengths, there is nothing better than having a visionary coach who can guide you through this process in a way that helps you connect with your talents on a deeper level and truly see how unique you really are. It's one thing to have your mom say you're beautiful or talented, but once you start hearing it from strangers, it gains more weight and has more power. By working with a coach, you can realize these insights faster and learn how to apply them in your business to achieve the success you desire.

Design your business selfishly, all about you, to let your inner light shine brightly.

Reflection question: What unique gifts, strengths, and talents do you have to share with the world?

The Inner Way – Listen to Your Body

"Insight is not a lightbulb that goes off inside our heads.
It is a flickering candle that can easily be snuffed out."
Malcolm Gladwell, *Blink: The Power of Thinking*
Without Thinking

If you aren't used to trusting your gut, listening to your intuition, and accepting that you already know the answers that you need, I completely understand where you are coming from and have struggled right there with you for years. At times, I still do, and I rely on several techniques to help me connect with my true self. As I mentioned previously, your inner voice needs to be the loudest in your head and, at times, it can have a lot of competition. If you have trouble hearing your inner voice or aren't sure what it sounds like, it's time to plug in an amplifier so that you can start to sense what feels right to you. Your inner voice can act as an effective filter and a confident guide for you to make sound decisions in your business.

To make room for your inner voice to speak up, experiment with the various techniques below to see what works best for you. Everyone is different, so what works for one person might not work for another. I invite you to keep trying and stay open to finding a clear connection that supports you. And know that it's okay if these suggestions sound crazy to you. You're here reading this book for a reason, so give these options a try to see what works best for you.

Muscle testing. In case you aren't familiar with kinesiology, I'll tell you that it's the study of the mechanics of body movement. The technique of muscle testing is derived from kinesiology and boils down to using your body to answer yes-or-no questions at a subconscious level. I'll cover it briefly here and I encourage you to research it more if it captures your interest.

At its most basic level, to start using muscle testing to answer simple questions, stand up with your feet flat on the floor and take a few deep breaths to relax your body. Be sure you're hydrated. Close your eyes. Feel free to put your hand on a chair or table for balance and safety. Then, out loud, ask your body to show you a "yes." Your head and torso will likely lean forward, backward, or make some other noticeable movement such that, when the request is repeated, gives a consistent response. Again, out loud, ask your body to show you a "no." Your head and torso will likely lean in an opposite direction from showing you a "yes." When the same request is repeated, you get a consistent response.

Note that for some people, this method doesn't work. If you're one of them, don't fret. It's often a sign that you don't trust yourself on a subconscious level. Contact me for more support around learning to trust yourself and unlocking the power of muscle testing.

You can use these physical "yes" and "no" responses to help answer questions ranging from "Should I have a peanut butter sandwich for lunch?" to "Am I ready to hire a personal assistant?" When you ask a question that isn't clear enough, your body might not move at all or might shift in another direction altogether to signify that the question is unclear. If that happens, try to simplify your question to elicit a more clear response.

Note that not every answer you get will be "correct." This isn't a foolproof method for connecting to your inner voice, as you can force the answer you desire if you so choose. This isn't something you take to Las Vegas and bet your life savings on at the roulette table. That said, it can be a powerful way to help you make decisions and get clear on what you want in your business. This is most accurate when you are grounded into your body, hydrated, and asking clear questions that are in the present moment.

Journaling. If you enjoy writing and find that journaling helps your ideas flow more freely, try journaling on a topic that you want more clarity around. Experiment with both broad and narrow topics to see what works best for you. While some people find that journaling freely offers the most clarity, others find that focusing on a specific topic or question is more fruitful. The simple act of writing down your thoughts can quiet the chaos of your mind and connect you more deeply with your inner wisdom and subconscious insights.

Writing a letter from one part of yourself to another part of yourself. If your faith leads you to believe in a higher power, here is a chance to write a letter from yourself to that higher power or anyone else for that matter. In turn, you can craft a response from that recipient to yourself. I've heard of people writing the response letter with their non-dominant hand to engage the opposite side of their brains. When I do this exercise, I often write to my spirit self, my core, or my soul to uncover answers to challenges or questions I'm facing at the time. The act of writing out my thoughts has produced powerful results along my journey.

Have a conversation with yourself. If you aren't much of a writer, you can have a chat with yourself in front of a mirror, while switching from one chair to another, by simply turning your head from one side to another, or putting on one hat to represent yourself and a different hat to connect with your inner wisdom.

Meditation. This is a hot-button word. If you don't like to "meditate," consider calling it "sitting quietly without distraction for five minutes and focusing on your breathing." That's all meditation is anyway. You can't do it wrong. If you get distracted, just start again. There is no need to beat yourself up for messing it up or not reaching someone else's idea of enlightenment. You can use guided meditations just as effectively as sitting in silence.

Movement. If sitting still doesn't inspire you, try a more active method of meditation. Take a walk. Go for a run. Clean your kitchen or scrub your floors. These simple actions can often quiet your mind long enough for your inner light to shine through and nudge you toward the answers you seek. Some people find the serenity of walking through a labyrinth in a quiet garden helps to clear the mind.

Draw. Another form of meditation involves drawing, doodling, coloring, or creating elaborate mandalas to occupy one part of your brain while quieting the other and allowing clarity to arise. If you have a coloring book and some crayons, give this a try. Again, don't worry that you're doing it wrong or your drawing isn't good enough. The point is to shift your brain into another gear so that clarity can slip in when you least expect it.

Make a decision. Sometimes, the best way to get clarity around a situation is to decide one way or the other and go about your day as though it's a done deal and see how it feels. Similarly, you can choose the alternative decision to see how that feels different in your body. Consider practicing on many smaller decisions to hone this skill further.

Connect to your body and your senses. Depending on where you are along your intuitive path, you may already know which of your senses offers the clearest response and accurate insights to support your decision-making and help you hear your true self. There are five main "clair" senses: clairvoyance (clear seeing), clairaudience (clear hearing), clairsentience (clear feeling), clairalience (clear smelling), clairgustance (clear tasting). The first three are more common and it's typical to have one that stands out stronger than the others. You might receive messages in your dreams or see numbers or symbols in your daily life that offer messages from loved ones. You might hear songs replayed in your head or hear messages guiding you to locate your misplaced car keys. You might feel like something is wrong without understanding how you know – for example, as a mother, you might intuitively "know" when your child is in danger. Less commonly, you might smell or taste something that gives you insights or reminds you of someone you know.

* * *

I encourage you to continue researching these methods for connecting with your true self if you aren't already advancing along your intuitive path. The more you allow your inner voice to be heard, the brighter your light can shine, and that brightness will directly translate into increased success in your business.

Reflection questions: Use your preferred intuitive method from above to review the talents you have identified so far and ask "Does and this resonate with me? Does this describe me well?"

Create Your Top Ten List

My hope for you is that by now some ideas for your unique talents have surfaced. It's time to gather your results and see what you've learned so far.

Create a list of your top ten talents and use your preferred intuitive method to check with your inner spirit to ensure that you're on the right track. By checking in with your body, you'll have more confidence in which talents feel "right" before you move on to the next step in the Process of ALLOWING Clarity. Remember that you're in control here.

Reflection question: What themes do you notice in your top ten true talents list?

Own Your True Talents

I wish I could tell you that simply identifying your true talents is enough but unfortunately, it isn't. You also need to own them.

Instead of brushing off compliments that come your way and trying not to be a braggart about your gifts, you need to embrace and accept them. Women are notorious for being worse than men when it comes to embracing their gifts and allowing their talents to shine. Instead of standing in the shadows and hiding your talents, give thanks for their role in your life and share them freely with others. How will anyone know that you are the best wedding planner in the area if you don't tell them how you just planned an amazing wedding?

We'll cover ways to talk about your true talents in Stage 2 of this book. Until then, start by owning your expertise.

Own Your Expertise

The challenge with being great at something is that you might not know how good you are until someone else tells you. That's what it's like to be an expert. You're so knowledgeable in your field that the work you do comes easily to you. Many times, you'll assume that everyone is great at balancing their checkbook, coordinating outfits, or planning amazing events. Once you realize that you are special and have true talents that others don't possess, you also need to accept that you are an expert.

You could be thinking, "Of course! I've been studying this topic my whole life and have years of experience with the degrees and certifications to back up my claim of expert status." But it's more likely that you're thinking the opposite: "I can't be an expert in this field. There are so many people out there who know more than me. They are the true experts." Or you have a case of not having arrived yet saying, "Once I have a degree in my field/more experience/another certification, then I can consider being an expert, but for right now I'm still learning."

The funny thing about becoming an expert is that there isn't a clear line you suddenly cross and "poof," you're magically an expert. What makes you an expert is knowing more than the people on the path behind you. If you're a mother who has given birth to a child, you're an expert to any woman who hasn't given birth because you have knowledge that she doesn't possess. That doesn't mean that you are an expert at delivering babies.

Being an expert simply means that you have knowledge to give about a topic that could help someone with less knowledge about it.

When you change how you view the term "expert," it's easier to see how it applies to you.

If owning your expertise and seeing how you can help others at this very moment in your business is something you struggle with, understand that it's normal to be stuck in this space. You're so close to your business that you can't always see what everyone else might think is obvious, until it is reflected to you. Allow space for your expertise to become clear as you work through this process.

Once you have identified your true talents, it's time to translate them into the design of your business. Consider how these true talents fit into your business.

Reflection questions: How can your unique strengths be incorporated to differentiate your business in the marketplace? How can your abilities be harnessed to provide superior service to your clients?

Summary Checklist

To get clear on how to allow your inner light to shine, gain clarity around who you are, identify your true talents, and own your expertise, be sure to answer the questions and complete the exercises listed below:

- Think of a time when you learned a great life lesson when something didn't work out as planned. What happened?
- Ask five people who know you well to honestly list your top five personality traits.
- List five topics you could talk about for hours or write a book about.
- Take a personality test.
- Which characteristics can combine into themes that will reveal your true talents?
- Pay attention and note compliments you receive.
- What unique gifts, strengths, and talents do you have to share with the world?
- Experiment with muscle testing to connect with your subconscious.
- Journal your thoughts to clear your mind and make space to allow insights.
- Write a letter from one part of yourself to another part of yourself.
- Have a conversation with yourself.
- Meditate for three minutes a day to center yourself and clear your mind.
- Move around to allow your thoughts to flow freely.

- Draw a picture or doodle to engage different parts of your brain.
- Make a decision and check in with your body to see if it feels right.
- Connect to your body. Observe and rank your "clair" senses.
- Use your preferred intuitive method from above to review the talents you have identified so far and ask yourself, "Does this resonate with me? Does this describe me well?"
- What themes do you notice in your top ten true talents list?
- How can your unique strengths be incorporated to differentiate your business in the marketplace? How can your abilities be harnessed to provide superior service to your clients?

As we continue the Process of ALLOWING Clarity, stay connected to your true self so that you remain in alignment with what you really want throughout the eight steps. When you feel more clear about who you are, and have identified your true talents, move on to the next step of Listening to Your Heart.

If you want more support around exploring and experimenting with this chapter's exercises, schedule a free Clarity Call (amandahyoung.com/free). I'll be glad to help you see more truth as you find out All About You.

Chapter 4 – Listen to Your Heart

"I can tell you that what you're looking for is already inside you."
Anne Lamott

ALLOWING – *L* is for *L*isten to Your Heart

The second step in the Process of ALLOWING Clarity is to Listen to Your Heart. When you live to serve others, you can easily confuse what you want in life with what others want for you. You might be used to others making decisions for you and nudging you in a direction they thought best suited you. As the leader of your life, and the leader of your business, it's time to give yourself permission to listen to your heart and do what you want to do. Selfishly design a business that you love.

The Seductive Shoulds

As entrepreneurs, following other people's advice is often used as a formula for success that guarantees you'll reach your goals. In your business, the "formula for success" trap can be disguised as Seductive Shoulds. These Shoulds remind me of the Sirens in Greek mythology who enticed sailors into dangerous waters with their beautiful voices, causing the sailors to shipwreck on their rocky shores and become trapped.

In your business, there may be times when you'll read an article that explains how Pinterest is the hot new way to attract clients to your business. Then you'll hear from a friend that they got a new client using Facebook ads. Later, it might be referrals from a networking group or an article in a local newspaper. The Seductive Shoulds will kick in and make you think that you *should* be doing more on Pinterest to get clients. You *should* be running an ad on Facebook to build your list. You *should* have a newsletter that you send out each week, and a blog to attract people to your website. You *should* also join your friend's networking group and write an article for a local newspaper while you're at it. You'll quickly become overwhelmed by the long list of things that you *should* be doing. After all, you're an entrepreneur and you *should* be serving your clients, creating better programs, keeping in touch with them more often, and making sure their invoices are current. But you *should* also be spending more time with your family, doing the laundry, eating healthy meals, and getting enough sleep.

These *shoulds* can be very seductive as they offer a false promise of making your life a little bit better in some way. Unfortunately, they come with hidden baggage that you might not realize you're carrying until it's too late. That baggage could be guilt that you aren't doing enough or that you aren't enough in some way. It could be doubt and confusion that leave you unable to make decisions. You could be wasting your precious energy on tasks that make you feel productive and appear busy but don't advance you toward your dreams. Oftentimes, the concealed baggage is a distracting detour sign that takes you hundreds of dollars and weeks away from your goal without you even noticing what's happened.

Speaking of detours, a client was referred to me because he thought he needed to rebrand his company. He liked helping homeowners figure out how to make their homes energy efficient, but he had it in his head that he should become a heating and cooling company that offered emergency repair services to get his foot in the door with prospective clients. He had spent months researching the heating and cooling industry and decided that the emergency repair service model was going to be the easiest way for him to attract clients. At our third meeting, I asked him to honestly say what he loved doing. He replied, "Renovating the apartments my family owns." As the answer fell from his mouth, he smiled at me and said, "Thanks for saving me $20,000 by telling me not to rebrand my business."

Somewhere during the process of becoming an entrepreneur, we may have accepted the idea that other people know what's best for us and we should follow a proven path to create a successful business. As entrepreneurs, we must challenge that thinking, reject the idea that anyone knows what's best for us better than we do, and lead ourselves, and our clients, down our own path to achieve our own goals. It is when you are selfish in your business that you can make the best decisions for the greatest good. After all, being a leader and blazing our own trails is what true entrepreneurship is all about. And that means following your heart.

Listen to Yourself

What are you – a busy, distracted, and overwhelmed entrepreneur – to do when all this chaos and indecision is buzzing around you, invading your space, and making you feel hopelessly lost in your business? Do this:

- Call for a time-out.
- Step back.
- Take a deep breath and ask yourself, "Is this what I really want?" Or, as one of my coaches put it, "Does this serve me well?"

When you combine these questions with the intuitive feedback you allow from your body, you can find the true answer quite easily. And that, my friend, is how you listen to your heart. You listen to yourself and what you want.

You can expose yourself to 20 different answers from 20 different people, all telling you what they think you *should* do. But, in the end, you are the one who needs to make the best decision for your situation. Even though you might doubt yourself at times, you must understand that *you* are the most qualified person to make decisions about *your* life.

That doesn't mean I want you to stop asking for advice or think you have to make decisions alone. It means that you can gather all the information you want to comfortably make an informed decision, and then allow space in your body to listen to what you, your soul, your spirit, your heart – whatever you want to call it – wants. Don't spend more time on social media or invest in a new website just because someone else said that's what you *should* do. Invest in yourself and your business in ways that you feel drawn to, connected to, and supported by. That's when you'll realize the true success of your dreams.

Business by Design

There are two ways to go about building your business: outward-facing, and inward-facing. When your business is outward-facing, you give what you think others need and they take what they want from you. When your business is inward-facing, you allow your gifts to shine while others are energized and inspired by your light.

Most of our businesses begin as outward-facing businesses that we blindly stumble through while desperately hoping things improve. Our clients ask us to help them with a challenge they are facing, and we offer them a solution. Our solution addresses their symptoms and, while it might not solve their problem, it improves their situation by pointing them in the right direction.

There comes a point when we realize our solutions aren't working as well as we had hoped. We aren't getting the traction and results we anticipated. And we aren't leading our clients to long-term solutions. That's the moment we realize we aren't in charge. The tail is wagging the dog. To get back in control, take the lead in our business, and create better results for our clients, we need to learn how to wag our own tails. The shift happens when we switch from an outward-facing business that we think is helping our clients, to an inward-facing business that is helping us intensify the power within us to create outstanding results for our clients. Instead of designing our business with others in mind, we need to design our business with our needs in mind, so that we can become the best version of ourselves and serve our clients from the highest level.

But what does that even mean, and how do we do it?

Find Your *Why*

Simon Sinek, author of *Start With Why: How Great Leaders Inspire Everyone to Take Action*, and famous for his TED Talk on the same topic, explains your *Why* as, "The purpose, cause, or belief that inspires you to do what you do." Finding your reason for being in business is key to your success. Two key points from his TED Talk were: "People don't buy what you do; they buy *why* you do it" and "The goal is not just to sell to people who need what you have. The goal is to sell to people who believe what you believe."

Why are you in business?

I'm in business to help entrepreneurs find easier ways to share their gifts with the world.

What do you believe?

I believe that it should be easy for entrepreneurs to market their businesses and achieve their goals when they have great gifts to offer that can truly help people. I believe the more clear entrepreneurs are around the purpose of their businesses, the more successful they will be and the greater their impact will be on the world.

Reflection questions: Why are you in business? What do you believe?

Digging Deeper

Instead of taking the first answer that comes to you for the questions above, I invite you to dig deeper. Repeat the same question ten times or until you feel like you've exhausted your answer and found the root of your reasoning. After each answer, ask yourself, "Why is that important?"

From the example above:

- Q: Why are you in business?
- A: I'm in business to help entrepreneurs and make marketing easier.
- Q: Why is that important?
- A: So they can be more successful and achieve their goals.
- Q: Why is that important?
- A: So they don't struggle in their businesses or experience prolonged financial strain.
- Q: Why is that important?
- A: So they don't feel like failures for not being able to attract clients to their businesses.
- Q: Why is that important?
- A: So they can spend less time marketing and more time making a difference.
- Q: Why is that important?
- A: So they can enjoy what they do with less stress and better results.
- Q: Why is that important?
- A: So they can find easier ways to share their gifts with the world.

- Q: Why is that important?
- A: So they aren't wasting time and money on marketing that doesn't align with their goals.
- Q: Why is that important?
- A: So they make smart marketing decisions instead of being taken advantage of.
- Q: Why is that important?
- A: So they don't feel so overwhelmed by their marketing.
- Q: Why is that important?
- A: So they are empowered to lead their clients in a way that makes a bigger impact.
- Q: Why is that important?
- A: So they can reinvest in causes that create lasting change in the world.

This technique of digging deeper and asking, "Why is that important?" can be used to help you become more clear on a variety of questions and issues beyond finding your *Why*. Give it a try to see what you uncover. Take any new insights a step further by asking yourself how your answers apply to your business. Are there changes you can make that support your reason for being in business?

Later on in this book, as we enter Stage 2 of the Process of ALLOWING Clarity and switch our focus to Communicating Clearly, you'll use the answers from this exercise to share your beliefs with the world and attract clients with the same beliefs.

Define Your Success

When it comes to reaching your goals and manifesting the life you desire, the popular marketing phrase "results may vary" comes to mind. The more clear and specific you are about what you want, the easier it is to receive it. When you don't have anything to aim for, it's hard to know when you've succeeded. While some entrepreneurs want to set goals and check them off a list as they are realized, others find the goals themselves to be limiting, stifling, and unsupportive. I invite you to let go of the rules around what makes a good goal and focus instead on the results and outcomes you want to achieve.

Success could mean that you attract $30,000, $50,000, or $100,000 to your business per year. Maybe your business is ready to hit the million-dollar mark. Having a specific revenue goal can be a strong motivation for some entrepreneurs and can be a sign of failure and a source of pressure for others. If you find the numbers to be more oppressive than inspiring, consider connecting less to an income number and more to a feeling or a milestone in your business that would warm your heart. Do you want to help 30 new clients learn how to eat healthier this year? Or is success defined by having an email newsletter audience of 1,000? Will you be successful in your business when you drop your kids off to school in a luxury car? Or when you are financially stable enough to make a $10,000 donation to your favorite charity?

By creating a vision for what you want your life to look like, how you want to feel supported by your business, and what change you want to inspire in your clients, you'll have a strong foundation to build the business of your dreams.

Reflection questions: How do you define your success? What does success look like to you? How do you want to feel? How will it feel when you have achieved something you set your sights on?

Allowing Abundance

Defining success and identifying outcomes in your business often brings up a lot of feelings around money and offers a real opportunity for you to clear out money beliefs that aren't serving you well. When your beliefs around wealth and abundance include a shortage or a limit to the number of resources available for everyone to enjoy, you block your wealth. If you don't think you are worthy of wealth, it will be hard for you to become wealthy. If you think wealthy people are all jerks, and you don't want to be a jerk, you might unknowingly be preventing your wealth.

The Law of Attraction, which is the concept that like attracts like, can be a powerful force in your business. Consider the rules you have created internally around money and how you can shift your beliefs to support your abundance. Your thoughts can be very powerful and when you think about money negatively, you risk blocking your abundance. Choose your thoughts carefully and be sure to ask for wealth to be attracted to you *with grace and ease* to prevent receiving wealth as a result of accidents or inheritances that aren't actually what you want.

Visualizing your wealth goals, repeating money mantras around abundance, and allowing yourself to embrace wealthy and luxurious lifestyles are all ways you can allow more abundance into your life as you design your business for success.

Investing in Outcomes

The word "sell" often brings up negative feelings and emotions. You might have stories you have created around the idea of selling yourself, your business, and your ideas. The key to selling is to shift your thinking from selling as something you do to an opportunity for others to take action to get the results they want. When you allow your clients to invest in an outcome they want through you, their outcome is set in motion and more likely to become a reality.

If you want to have your taxes done in a way that reduces your overall tax bill while protecting you from a painful audit process, your accountant has an opportunity for you to take action (hire her) to get the results you want (taxes done correctly by a professional). She doesn't have to "sell" her services. She does need to present them to you in a way that aligns with your objectives. If she presents them in a way that matches what you want, you have the opportunity to invest in the outcome you desire. It's that easy.

When you move away from the idea of sales being slimy and release the idea that you need to *convince* your clients to buy your services, you free up more positive energy around selling that can dramatically change your business. You can exhaust yourself chasing clients, or you can invite and allow clients to work with you. They are two very different ways to pursue similar outcomes and you'll find the latter energy to be most effective. Later in this book, we'll focus on how to communicate your services in a well-crafted offer that easily attracts more of the right clients to your business.

Design Your Business

Once you clearly understand your true reason for why you are in business, you can create an inward-facing business to support your dreams that align with your true talents. To design an inward-facing business, you'll intentionally focus on what you want. Combine your true talents with your *Why* to design a framework that supports your goals.

For example, my client Samantha knew that she had a true talent for planning memorable family vacations and getting her clients great deals. She was in business because she was tired of seeing travelers overpay and she wanted to find a way to support charities through her work. To design her business, she harnessed her talent for planning family vacations and created a company where she donates a portion of her commission back to the charity of her client's choice. Her clients would pay the commission if they booked with her or used a travel website themselves. With her help, they can save money, make a generous donation, and have the support of an industry expert.

When you make time to take a step back and create a vision for your business, it's easy to take deliberate action toward your goals instead of wandering around in hopes that you stumble upon success. Success isn't something you typically fall into, but it is the result of thoughtful planning, consistent pursuit, and deliberate action. We'll cover having a clear action plan later in this book. Until then, think about how your true talents can be aligned with your *Why* to build a business that helps you reach the results you desire.

Summary Checklist

To listen to your heart and get clear on why you're in business, what you want your business to be, and how you can achieve your outcomes, complete the exercises listed below:

- Make a list of things you think you *should* be doing. Then list why you feel that way and who thinks you should do each item listed.
- Create a vision board using photos, phrases, and images that inspire you and represent the results you want to achieve.
- Why are you in business? What do you believe?
- How do you define your success? What does success look like to you? How do you want to feel? How will it feel when you have achieved something you set your sights on?

- Write a wish list of three outcomes that you want to achieve in the areas of business, relationships, health, happiness, and wealth. Follow each with the support you need to achieve each result.
- Visualize that your results have been achieved by stepping into an imaginary time machine and fast-forwarding six months or a year from now and having a party to celebrate your achievements. Notice who is in attendance, what you are celebrating, and how you feel.
- Think about a time when you did something you wanted to do and how it felt to achieve that outcome. How would you describe that feeling? How can you recreate that feeling in your business?

Chapter 5 – Love Your Clients

"The aim of marketing is to know and understand the customer so well the product or service fits him and sells itself."
Peter Drucker

ALLOWING – *L* is for *Love* Your Clients

To truly love your clients, you need to set boundaries and get clarity around who you want to work with, what they want, what they need, and where to find them. You can waste a lot of time, money, and energy chasing after clients, or you can allow clients to find you and want your services by speaking in a way that connects with them on a deeper level and offers a solution they want.

The third step in the Process of ALLOWING Clarity is to Love Your Clients. By working with your favorite clients, you will do better work, have more fun, and achieve better results. When you work with clients who aren't ideal, you run the risk of wavering from your path, being tempted by money, or being distracted by an easier route that pulls you away from what you really want.

Early on in your business, it's normal to not know who you want to work with right away. And, as your business evolves, your perfect clients will evolve, too.

Embracing this process and allowing space to make mistakes and learn along the way is critical to your success.

My hope for you is to be able to describe your favorite client and what they want in specific detail so that you can identify them easily. You'll get to know them on a deeper level so that you have keen insights into how they struggle and can offer smart solutions to help them. We will build up your understanding of who you want to work with in the second stage of this book when we discuss ways to craft your marketing messages to speak directly to the clients you want to work with most.

Anyone with a Pulse

If you have ever been to a networking group where everyone goes around the table taking turns pitching their business and describing who they want to work with, you've likely heard someone say, "A good referral for me is anyone with a pulse." Whenever this happens, I cringe inside and my heart aches for that person. Do they really want me to refer them to my five-year-old son? Would they be able to serve someone diagnosed with dementia? Or do they want someone who is recently married and about to buy their first home?

Not to pick on the insurance industry, but they tend to be some of the worst offenders when it comes to overgeneralizing the customers they work with because they can serve so many people at different life stages. It's a common trap for financial planners and advisors, too. We'll address how to deal with having multiple target markets later in this chapter, but I want you to understand how to focus on one small target first.

Hearing someone say they want to serve "anyone with a pulse" is the kiss of death when it comes to asking for referrals because our brains can't sort the list of people we have connections with down into a manageable list of people to recommend.

If I say, "A good referral for me is a college student currently renting an apartment," you might think of three people you know who fit that description. If I'm an insurance agent selling rental insurance policies, then those college students would have a high potential for being some of my favorite clients. Even better would be "a high-school graduate heading off to college and renting their first apartment." Why? Because they probably don't know they should have rental insurance and likely don't have an insurance agent that they prefer. By being more specific, you've narrowed your target list even further and, in doing so, created leads that are better aligned with your services.

Reflection question: Think about the example above and everyone you know. Who could you refer to our insurance agent? How many people would you be able to refer to them if they asked you for a) anyone with a pulse or b) a college student currently renting an apartment or c) a high-school graduate heading off to college and renting their first apartment?

Narrow Your Target

In traditional marketing courses, you are trained to cast the widest net possible to capture enough leads to make your business successful. Once you capture a massive quantity of leads, you then need to sort through them all to find the ones that will be a good fit and be most likely to actually buy from you. You start with a really big ocean of fish, cast a wide net to capture as many fish as possible, filter through them to find all of the tuna fish, and finally, sort them out into the more specific yellowfin tuna that you are most equipped to serve.

If you have 20 species of fish in your wide net and you're only able to serve the yellowfin tuna fish really well, you've just wasted a lot of time, money, and resources catching the other 19 types of fish in your wide net. The entire process is incredibly wasteful.

Wouldn't you rather skip over all that extra work, time, money, and resources spent on all those steps and cast a net that only caught yellowfin tuna? Do you see how you can save a lot of time, money, and resources by customizing your net to narrow your focus and choose a specific group of clients to serve?

Entrepreneurs often start out willing to help anyone who remotely fits their target client because they don't have the experience to know who they really enjoy working with or who they are best equipped to help. Some entrepreneurs fear that narrowing their target too much will result in not having any clients. In practice, the opposite is true. When you are more specific about who you work with and what you can do for them, you can connect with them on a deeper level and attract more people who are facing similar issues.

That said, while it's great to be specific, there is also a time and place where it's okay to be vague. I used to think that I had to be able to sort my clients into one tidy category. They were all going to be architects, or nonprofit organizations, or wealthy visionaries revolutionizing their industries. When I didn't immediately find a category that all my early clients fit into, I was sure I was failing to find my niche and ruining any chance I had at success. What I realized was that the purpose of this process is less about finding my perfect target market and more about finding the common outcome the people I attract all want.

You're Not Being Exclusive

When you cast a smaller net and catch clients one at a time, or in small groups, you can provide high-quality service and personalized attention that creates lasting results. As a small business owner, bigger isn't always better when you aren't set up to manage large quantities of clients at one time.

The challenge in narrowing your target is allowing yourself to trust the process and understand that having one favorite client that you solely focus on will create the space for people with similar struggles to relate to you better. Marketing to one individual will help you connect on a deeper level with hundreds of people. Even if you select one person who happens to be a woman trying to find a better way to manage her money so that she has enough wealth for retirement, you'll attract men who also want a better way to manage their money to enjoy better vacations.

Just like declaring your favorite food is 70-percent dark chocolate with crushed almonds, you aren't announcing that you'll never enjoy a cheddar cheeseburger again. It just means that your friends will be more likely to offer you dark chocolate with almonds for dessert because you've clearly stated your desires. Do the same in your business and you'll realize spectacular results.

Toss Traditional Target Markets

Most programs that offer marketing advice start with traditional target marketing that sorts prospective clients based on demographics, including sex, age, income, education level, nationality, and religion. The challenge arises when you serve clients who don't all check the same boxes; they don't fit into a tight age range, have different education levels, and are of different sexes. While demographics can narrow your target in some cases, it can leave you feeling really lost in others.

That's when psychographics come into play. Psychographics include your prospective clients' values, opinions, and interests. In many cases, you can find a common thread among your favorite clients by looking at what they want, need, desire, and fear. By combining any insights gained from reviewing a handful of your favorite clients, you can string together patterns that will help you find prospective clients more easily. If you know they all have golden retrievers as members of their families, you can easily find them buying pet food, visiting veterinarians, and donating to golden retriever rescue organizations. For those of you who don't have it this easy and struggle to identify your favorite clients clearly, don't worry. We have several other ways to help you narrow your focus.

Reflection questions: How would you describe your favorite client in terms of demographics? What do they want? What do they actually need? What do they dream about and desire? What do they fear? What do your favorite clients have in common?

Identify Your Favorite Client

Instead of finding a group of people that you can gather together, label, and call your target market, you can flip the process on its head and pinpoint a single person to represent your favorite clients. Even if you do find a traditional target market that fits neatly into a box and offers a clear description of who you work with, finding your favorite clients by focusing on a single client you love can provide priceless insights to support your success.

To identify your favorite client, here are a few exercises to try:

Get ready. Take a moment to connect with your body. Take a few deep breaths to clear your head. Grab a notebook to record any insights that arise. Allow yourself to let go of what you think your favorite client should be, or what characteristics they might have that would make you more money. Release your preconceived notions and start with a blank slate. Consider what characteristics you like most and want to work with. If you need to take a minute to write down what you think they *should* be like, I encourage you to do so and to note *why* you feel that way. Once you have moved all of the preconceptions out of the way, you'll be free to embrace your inner preferences.

A younger you. Ask yourself if you were your own favorite client a few years ago. Are you looking back and helping people just like you? Maybe you're a mom who struggled to find a job that paid well with the flexibility to support your family and you now want to help other moms find fulfilling work.

A former client. If a former you isn't your current favorite client, is there a real person you have worked with or would like to work with? Describe that person in depth. Allow them to represent your favorite client. Describe everything you can about them. Was there a client you worked with who absorbed all of your advice, implemented your ideas, and got great results? Maybe you have two or three of those clients that you can combine to paint a descriptive picture of your favorite client: one who paid on time, another who provided testimonials proving how successful your work together was, and a third who was willing to try a new software that would improve their processes.

A list of qualities. Create a list of everything you can think of that you do and don't want in a client. Maybe you want them to join you for meetings in exotic locations. Maybe you don't want to travel at all. You might want them to pay upfront and commit to working with you for a minimum of six months. By listing out the traits you don't want from your favorite clients, you can start to outline the boundaries you need to establish in your business.

Write a description. Describe your favorite client specifically in two paragraphs. Give them a name and detail their struggles, hopes, and desires. What do they need help with the most? And what would they gladly pay someone to help them fix? Is there a problem they have that is causing them pain? What have they tried to do about it that has or hasn't worked?

Boil it down to one line. Once you have an idea of who they are and what they struggle with, edit your two-paragraph description down to one line that captures their essence. If you spoke to your neighbor about this person, how would you describe them?

List their symptoms. Identify symptoms your favorite client would have before they hire you. Would they say something to their friends like, "I have had so much trouble finding someone responsible to take care of my dog while I'm at work"? Would they complain about a fear they have, like "It feels like I'm busy all of the time but I'm not getting anything done or making any progress"? Is their closet packed full of clothing that doesn't fit? Do they wonder if they will ever be able to find a trustworthy assistant? Can you identify their symptoms by listing ways your services can help them?

Having Multiple Favorites

What if your client exploration still turns up more than one favorite client? In the earlier example where people make the mistake of saying that a good referral is "anyone with a pulse," they tend to be offering more than one service to a variety of clients and they suffer from a lack of clarity. While they think that they can work with anyone, the reality is that if someone walks into their office, they will have specific services to offer them.

Going back to the insurance example: a renter will need rental insurance coverage and a homeowner needs homeowners' insurance. A young woman might need health insurance with maternity coverage while a man won't.

Instead of using the same brush to paint one broad stroke that covers everyone you serve, paint one person and clearly describe them individually. You can set a different favorite client to focus on each week or month. This works even better when you know your audience and can talk about one of your favorite clients that your audience is most likely to know. A room full of moms of high-school-age children may respond better to your request to connect with new college students who are renting their first apartments than first-time homebuyers.

If you offer a menu of business services that build on one another, pick the foundational service to start with and lead into the others over time. If individual health insurance leads to life insurance, start with your favorite clients for individual health insurance.

Allowing the Shift

Once you have a clear understanding of who you want to work with, who you don't want to work with, and how to identify them based on the symptoms they are experiencing, it's much easier to create a customized "net" to catch your favorite clients. And at this point, it no longer resembles a net at all, because you won't have to capture and convince clients to work with you. Instead, it's like you're putting out a buffet of delicious treats for your favorite clients to enjoy while they are nourished by your services and benefit from the gifts you have to offer. They will be magnetically attracted to your business when you allow yourself to get clear on who your favorite clients are and how you can serve them best. Your energy in your business will shift from needing to find clients to allowing clients to find you.

Ditch the Drag

In middle school, I was on the county swim team for the summer. During practice, the serious swimmers would wear their old, holey swimsuits over their regular suits to increase the resistance they encountered as they glided through the water. By practicing with the extra drag, they became stronger, faster swimmers. On race days, they would only wear their best swimsuit to perform their fastest time.

As an entrepreneur, having clients who aren't your favorite can create a similar effect of drag on your business. Except the bad clients aren't always making you stronger, faster, or better. In most cases, they are just slowing you down, causing you pain, and draining your energy in ways that aren't helpful to your business or theirs. Ditch the drag. Cut them loose and focus on your favorite clients. Doing so will allow space in your business for your best clients to break free and create amazing results instead of weighing you down to invest most of your time on the clients who aren't ideal.

While bad clients can be obvious if you dread meetings with them, can't wait to end your phone calls, avoid doing work for them, and put off your appointments as long as possible, they can also be disguised as favorite clients. In some cases, you might be willing to tolerate more of their less-than-perfect traits because they pay well or you think they could lead to more clients along the way.

Be sure to review your clients on an ongoing basis to ensure that you really are working with your favorite clients, and not clients that you've settled for until the really good ones come along. By firing the less ideal clients in your business, you open yourself up and create space for the amazing clients to join you. Allow yourself to stay true to your business and *love your clients*.

Reflection questions: Review the description of your favorite client. How does the idea of helping them feel? What reaction does it create in your body?

Summary Checklist

It's important to know as much as you can about your ideal client so that you can attract the clients you love and most want to serve.

- How would you describe your favorite client in terms of demographics? What do they want? What do they actually need? What do they dream about and desire? What do they fear? What do your favorite clients have in common?
- Is it possible that you were your own ideal client a few years ago?
- Is there a real person you have worked with or would like to work with?
- Create lists of everything you can think of that you do and don't want in a client.
- Describe your favorite client specifically in two paragraphs.
- Edit your two-paragraph description down to one line that captures their essence.
- Identify symptoms your favorite client would have before they hire you.
- Review the description of your favorite client. Do you want to work with this person?
- How does the idea of helping your favorite client feel? What reaction does it create in your body?

Throughout the Process of ALLOWING Clarity, stay connected to your true self so that you remain in alignment with who you want to work with.

If you want more support around exploring and experimenting with this chapter's exercises, schedule a free Clarity Call (amandahyoung.com/free). I'll be happy to help you identify and gain insights into your favorite clients.

Chapter 6 – Offer to Lead

*"I'm gonna *make* him an *offer* he *can't refuse*."*
Don Corleone in *The Godfather*

ALLOWING – *O* is for *O*ffer to Lead

The fourth step in the Process of ALLOWING Clarity is to Offer to Lead. It is the last step that focuses on designing your business selfishly. In this step, you'll continue to connect to your inner self and listen to your heart as you embrace your role as a leader to create clear offers that are uniquely positioned to support your clients and deliver the results they desire. When you lead your favorite clients through your process and offer opportunities that play to your strengths, you can be of service to them in the best possible way.

Lead Your Clients

In partner dancing, there are two roles: the leader and the follower. Both are equally important, with the lead partner deciding the direction you'll take and the moves you'll make and the following partner being patient, available, and trusting their lead. Both partners need to maintain a strong frame, communicate clearly, and work together for the dance to be successful.

The same principles apply to your business. When I first started as an entrepreneur, I tried to be a leader and a follower at the same time. I wanted to please my clients by doing anything they needed that I was capable of doing. It took a few tough projects and lost clients to realize that by reacting to what I thought my clients wanted from me, I wasn't being the leader they needed me to be. When you offer to lead, the services you provide can be of incredible value to your clients. By standing up, showing them your process, guiding them through your system, and supporting them along the way, you offer an opportunity to achieve the outcome they desire.

Know What You Offer

To craft an offer that your clients want, know what outcomes you're selling. What problem are you solving for your clients? If you can't clearly see their problem, it might help to think of the outcome you provide as the opportunity you present to them. Is there an outcome your clients want? If you are a home energy performance specialist, your client's problem could be that their heating system is outdated and they are spending too much money, and energy, to heat their home. You could offer them the opportunity to conserve energy and lower their heating bills. Maybe their system is up-to-date but they want an outcome where their home is a consistent temperature from the basement to the second story so they don't need to add or remove clothing each time they move from floor to floor. When you can clearly describe the challenge they are facing and the outcome you offer, it will be easier for your clients to invest in your services and the results they want.

Before crafting an offer for your prospective clients, you need to clearly understand what they want and know that you can deliver that outcome to them. The two examples listed above would each lead to a different offer because the results differ. The first client wants a more energy-efficient system. The second client wants to precisely control the temperature in their home.

You might be able to list out a dozen problems, opportunities, or outcomes that your clients want. Or you'll struggle to find one. Either way, what matters most is that you can offer them a solution that works.

To select the solution that works best, you need to answer a few questions: Can you solve their problem? Do you have a solution that works well enough to promise them an outcome they will be happy with? Does your solution meet their needs? Is this work that you want to be doing? Does it align with your true talents? Can your intuition confirm that this is work you want to be doing? Based on your education, experience, certifications, and expertise, are you qualified to help them?

If you are unsure about your answers, keep working on this. Set aside time to quiet your mind and your body and ask those questions. Revisit the exercises in the second step – Listen to Your Heart – and journal or talk through these ideas to get the clarity you need to move forward confidently. It's okay if you don't have answers right now. They can take time and they can change as your business evolves. You can always come back to this process to check in on your business down the road to see how aligned you are with your true self.

Reflection questions: What problems does your ideal client need help with? How can you provide a solution to their problem? Does what you offer meet their needs? Do you want to provide this solution to them? Are you qualified to provide this solution for them?

Your Signature Process

Starting in your business, you might not have a system in place that you can guide your clients through right away. You may need some practice to figure things out, but after a while, you'll start to see patterns emerge from the clients you work with. You'll have the same conversations with them about how you work, what they need to know, and how they can enhance their results. The more experience you have with your clients, the easier it will be to create a process that leads your desired clients to their desired results. Instead of reacting to what they think they want, you'll lead them through a process that gives them what they need.

Your clients might want someone to give them all the answers and tell them what to do in their business, but they need to learn to listen to the answers they hold deep inside their inner selves. You might start off thinking you're helping them by giving them all the answers they want, but they will question the answers you give them until you lead them through a process of self-discovery where they arrive at the answers themselves in a way that feels aligned with the essence of their being.

To create your signature process, lay out the steps you take all your clients through to help them get the outcome they desire. If they want to be less stressed about coordinating an outfit before work each morning, what steps can you lead them through to offer them an opportunity to wake up confident, knowing they have an outfit planned and easy to find that will look and feel great the moment they put it on.

Reflection question: What are the steps you can lead your clients through to deliver the results they want?

Describe the Benefits

When clients work with you, what happens to them during the process? Is there a transformation that takes place? If you're a wedding planner, will they experience the wedding of their dreams without exceeding their budget? If you're a financial planner, will they be able to retire confidently knowing that they have enough money to travel the world and afford quality in-home care as they age? What's going to change as a result of working with you?

Instead of becoming a stressed-out bridezilla too busy hosting the wedding to enjoy the wedding, your client could be the most beautiful guest at a party celebrating her marriage. Instead of your client worrying about whether they can afford to travel or to get quality long-term care once they retire, they'll know their investments are secure and plentiful enough to support the retirement of their dreams.

The transformations your clients go through and the results they receive are the benefits you offer. The specifics of this may not be obvious to you at first, or the obvious results might not seem all that important to you. From your client's perspective, why does each benefit you offer matter? You can often answer this question by listing your benefit and adding "so that..." and finishing the sentence to clarify why it's important for your clients to receive that specific result.

You can refer to Chapter 3, regarding finding your *Why*, for help with digging deeper into why your offerings and their benefits matter. To uncover your client's true benefits and reasons for wanting them, ask yourself, "What is the change they realize? Why does that change matter?" And then take that answer one step further by asking, "And why does *that* change matter?" When you feel like you have identified the true benefits your favorite clients want, ask a few of them for feedback and confirmation.

Reflection questions: What happens to your clients during your process? What is the transformation that takes place? Why does that change matter? Why is that important to them? What are five benefits your clients receive from working with you?

Sell the Outcome

A lot can go into determining the cost of an offer. To muddy the waters further, the conflicting advice on this subject can be overwhelming. Determining the price of your services will ultimately be decided by trial and error and learning what you are comfortable with. To get you started, here are a few things to consider.

Don't charge by the hour, charge by the outcome. When you charge by the hour, you limit the value of your work and can be punished for working fast. When you charge by the outcome, you can add value through your expertise, tools you offer to help your clients achieve their desired results, the chance to belong to a like-minded community, and the support you offer throughout the process.

Consider the perceived value. If you offer a life-changing program for 20 dollars, your prospects might think it's too good to be true. If your price is the highest in the marketplace, you might be seen as the best in your industry. If your price is the lowest, they might think they are getting a good value or they might question the quality of the results you claim to deliver. The price you charge needs to be equal to the price your ideal clients are willing to pay.

How much is your outcome worth to your client? A way to determine your pricing is to ask yourself what the outcome you can deliver to your client is worth. If working with you will save your client $100,000 this year, or help them increase their revenues by that amount, they might be willing to pay you $20,000 to achieve that outcome. If your outcome doesn't translate directly into income or tangible results, what is the value of saving them a week's worth of time or preventing them from being stuck in a contract that cripples their business? That has real value and is something you can charge for accordingly.

Allow them to invest in their results. Don't give your services away for free. Instead, offer a sales process that guides your prospective clients to see the value in working with you and what their life could look like after getting the results you can help them achieve. When you allow your clients to invest in you, you allow them to invest in their own results. They invest in themselves through you. If they say "yes" to your offer, that simple act of committing to working with you will help them achieve the results they desire. They are putting their energy and intention into working with you. If they say "no" to your offer, then they don't want the result you are offering, or not right now. Allow them to decide if they are ready to make the change you're offering to help them make. Ask clients who say "no" to your offer how they plan to solve their problem without you. If they truly aren't ready to invest in working with you, let them go.

When in doubt, raise your price. Most entrepreneurs err on the side of offering their services too cheaply, for fear that no one will buy. What they often overlook is the effect that their low pricing has on the perceived value of their services. Low prices could mean your clients are getting a great deal, or it could mean they are getting low-quality services according to the adage that "you get what you pay for."

Perception is everything, and it is easier to reduce your price, offer a discount, or add a bonus to your offering to sweeten an offer and increase its perceived value. If a client wants what you have, chances are they are willing to pay for it. If you are in a highly competitive and price-conscious industry, consider adding value in creative ways that don't cost you anything but that help your clients, while differentiating yourself using your true talents instead of lowering your price or competing on price alone.

Craft an Offer

Once you have answered the questions above, feel confident that you can solve your client's problem effectively, and can describe the benefits your clients receive from working with you, you're ready to craft an offer. Your offer will be similar to the format of a party invitation that includes the who, what, where, why, and how of an event. Answering these six questions can help:

Who is the offer for? These are your favorite clients, the ones you defined in the third step, Love Your Clients. Make this description specific and clearly identify who you want to work with. Note that if you sell your services to one audience (parents) but provide your service to another audience (their children), like in the example below, be sure to write your offer to the audience who is buying.

Parents of active school-age children on the 500 block of Main Street who like playing with water balloons and having fun with their neighbors.

What are the results they get? These are the benefits your favorite clients receive and why they matter. Your offer serves as an opportunity to address doubts your clients might have. If they fear that your services cost too much, won't work for their unique situation, or will take too long to reap the full benefits, you can speak to those concerns as you outline your offer.

The opportunity for your child to get out of the house, play with their neighbors in a safe and supervised environment, have fun, learn how to launch water balloons, cool off during the summer, and take home a personalized water sprayer, so that they can make new friends and be part of our neighborhood community.

Why should they do this now? To inspire your clients to take action, speak to their inner motivation. People don't want to miss out on great opportunities. When you limit the number of spaces or offer your services for a limited time, you create scarcity. This is why concert tickets sell out and unique venues are quickly filled. You can offer exclusivity to let your clients know they are special to be receiving this offer.

This party only happens once a year and is limited to 20 kids.

What does it include? These are the features and details of your offer. How long will you work together? How much time will you spend with your clients? What training will you provide? What tools will they have access to? Will they be part of a community or group that can support them during this process?

Your children will have unlimited access to water and balloons, a water sprayer with their name on it, the entire street blocked off from traffic, three hours to soak their friends, a variety of allergy-free foods, balloon-tying lessons, rapid-balloon-filling hoses, and adult supervision, so you can rest easy knowing your kids are safe.

How much does it cost? Price your offer at an amount you are comfortable saying out loud and that doesn't feel like you're being ridiculous but does feel like you're venturing slightly out of your comfort zone.

Your investment for our neighborhood summer adventure is twenty dollars per child and includes a their own personalized water sprayer, 500 balloons, and a large variety of allergy free snacks and healthy drinks.

What do they need to do? This is the call to action. Every offer you make needs to have a single, clear call to action. What do you want them to do next? Buy your program, contact you for a free consultation, apply to work with you, or sign up for your newsletter? While this may be the final step in the offer process, it is often overlooked as an opportunity to get clients on the phone so you can see for yourself if they'd be a good fit for you. Once you are on a call, you can lead them through a more personal description of your process to show them how you work and what they can expect from you. Carefully consider what one action you need your clients to take to move closer to working with you.

RSVP to 555-1111 by noon on Friday to reserve your child's space.

Simplify the Process

It's often said that, "A confused client never buys." If you think about a time when you wanted to buy something, had cash in hand, but couldn't figure out how to buy it, or couldn't find what you needed to do to move forward, you'll know how that feels. Part of leading your clients to decide to work with you is creating a simple process for them to follow to buy from you.

A friend of mine has a small business making homemade face and hand lotions out of her home. She added me to her mailing list and sent out emails telling me about the batches she would be making that month and offering them for sale in advance. To place an order, I had to email her for an order form, wait for it to be sent to me, fill it out, and then send it back to her so she could make the products for me. The process wasn't easy and left so much room for the emails to get messed up that I didn't bother to place an order, despite it being winter and my hands desperately needing the relief her products would provide.

With a simple tweak in her process – in this case, linking directly to the order form from her original email and using an automated shopping cart system – she streamlined the process and saved herself time while providing better customer service and increasing her sales.

An easier process might not always be obvious to you, but if you ask your clients for suggestions, or work with a business coach to tweak your process, you can realize amazing results. Make it easy for your clients to buy from you by putting systems in place that streamline your process.

Reflection questions: Think of a time when you wanted to buy something but you didn't know how, like a service you wanted, but then didn't buy. Why did you get stuck? How might your prospective clients get stuck in trying to buy from you? How can you streamline your sales process to make it easier for your clients to buy from you?

Gain Confidence

The online business landscape can be misleading these days. The rise of so many success stories of people who appear to have become millionaires overnight can leave the rest of us wondering what we are doing wrong.

In marketing, perception is everything. How you are perceived by your prospective clients can make or break your business. That said, while those apparent overnight millionaire entrepreneurs may be considered successful, they didn't all start that way.

Just like you and I, they all had to grow their businesses one step at a time. They tried and failed along the way, but they learned from their failures and gained confidence with each attempt they made. They didn't start their businesses knowing how to attract clients, offer webinars, or host sold-out seminars. They figured things out and tried until they found what worked for them and their ideal clients.

When making an offer to your prospective clients, do so knowing that most of the offers you make won't be wildly successful. You still need to make them, though, because you need to use them as your testing ground. Did the first pie you ever baked turn out to be perfect? Probably not. But each time you baked another pie, you learned something new and tweaked the recipe to make it better and then even better. Even the best pastry chefs botch a pie occasionally. It's natural. Accept that you'll mess things up and your offers won't always go as planned.

The keys to your success are testing things out, asking for feedback, trying new things, and homing in on an offer that speaks to your audience – and repeating that process until you've found the right mix of ingredients. When you've done that, you know you're ready and can confidently host a bake sale. Until then, celebrate the small victories along the way and add them up. Consider each new experience as a confidence booster as you get closer and closer to your dream.

Reflection questions: What's not working about your offer? What could you tweak to make it work better? Who could you ask for feedback? What confidence level do you exude? How do your prospects perceive you?

Maintain Your Focus

In yoga, the purpose is to connect with your body and get what you need from each pose. You are encouraged to listen to your body, know your limits, breathe into any discomfort, and engage safely, all while challenging yourself to allow your practice to provide what you need at that moment. You can set an intention at the beginning of each class. Maybe today you need to relax and release stress. Or maybe you need an energetic boost. Or maybe you need space to reconnect with your body and clear your mind. Whatever your reason, yoga is meant to be a solitary practice that benefits you and you alone.

During a yoga class at my local gym one day, I noticed that I constantly scanned the room to see who was moving deeper into poses than I was. I tried to find someone who wasn't holding their poses as long as I was or who wasn't challenging themselves with the advanced poses. It was at that moment that I realized my yoga practice wasn't about me but had become competitive yoga. I was stretching my body too far, holding the poses too long, and damaging my muscles in the process. In wanting to be the best yogi in the class, I was completely missing the point of why I was there in the first place. It was *my* yoga practice. I was the one who was supposed to be benefiting from my time on the mat. I wasn't being selfish in my yoga practice and it wasn't supporting my needs. I quit the class and went back to doing yoga at home, in private, where I could get out of the competitive mindset and focus on myself and my needs.

Distractions come in many forms as you build your business. Part of staying selfish during this process is maintaining your focus on what you want so that you don't end up having to completely rebuild your business from scratch because you followed someone else's dream. Instead of getting a law degree because your dad always wanted to be an attorney, follow your heart to your own dream. Instead of focusing your yoga practice on what everyone else is doing, focus on what you need. Instead of building a business where you offer your clients what you think you should be offering, offer them what they need that you can deliver.

Permission to Pivot

Throughout your business, you'll likely be tempted to change factors that seem like they're not working. Do you want to shift your definition of who your favorite clients are because you think they will be more fun to work with than your current clients? Maybe you want to create a different offer to support a subset of your clients and fill in a gap in the marketplace? If so, be sure to check with your inner self to confirm that's the right move for you. If it feels right, test it out. For small tweaks to your business, you can typically offer a pilot program with discounted pricing to see how your clients react to it and if it works. However, there may come a time in your business when the offers you are putting out aren't working and you aren't gaining any traction. Instead of giving up altogether, consider pivoting.

In his book *The Lean Startup*, Eric Reis explains the concept of a minimum viable product (MVP). It's the minimum offer you can deliver to still make a sale and get people interested in what you have to offer. If you're a bookkeeper, you might offer to enter a small business owner's expenses into their accounting software. If you can find clients who want to pay you for that service, you have a successful MVP. After offering that service for six months, you might realize that your heart isn't in it, it doesn't pay well enough to cover your expenses, and you really want to be offering a comprehensive service instead. At that point, you can "pivot" your business.

Pivoting means shift substantially in another direction. It involves putting a new spin on things and changing up your offerings, but without recreating your whole business.

A woman I met started her business teaching foreign languages to individual students in small private groups. In time, her business pivoted to offer classroom language services to private schools. A decade later, she was considering letting go of the individual private lessons so she could focus all her efforts on expanding her classroom offerings. To successfully pivot, she needed to give herself permission to change her mind from the original intention she had set for her business and focus on what was working successfully.

Reflection questions: What could a pivot do for your business? What could a pivot do for your clients? Do you feel like you need permission to pivot your business? What if you had that permission? What do you need for it to be okay to let go of offers in your business that aren't working and explore pivoting?

Reassure Your Ego

If, at this point, the voice in your head is telling you that you're a fraud, and you're asking yourself, "Who am I to be doing this work?", acknowledge your ego for trying to keep you safe by keeping you stuck where you are. By giving your ego a simple reply, like, "Your concern has been noted," or some other reassuring comment, you can let your inner critic know that it has been heard. Then it will be more likely to step back so you can move forward.

In the next step in the Process of ALLOWING Clarity, you'll learn to write your pitch.

Summary Checklist

To lead your clients through your process and create an offer that provides a lasting change in their lives, answer these questions and complete these exercises:

- What problems does your favorite client need help with? How can you provide a solution to their problems?
- What are steps you can lead your clients through to deliver the results they want?
- Does what you offer meet your clients' needs?
- Do you want to provide this solution to them? Are you qualified to provide this solution for them?
- What happens to your clients during your process? What is the transformation that takes place? Why does that change matter? Why is that important to them?
- What are five benefits your clients receive from working with you?
- What is the perceived value of your offer? How much is your outcome worth to your client? How can you charge your clients based on the outcome you deliver?
- How can you adjust your sales process to lead your prospects to easily invest in their outcomes through you?

- Would raising the price of your offer make sense?
- Craft your offer:
  - Who is the offer for?
  - What are the results they get?
  - Why should they do this now?
  - What does it include?
  - How much does it cost?
  - What do they need to do?
- Think of a time when you wanted to buy something but you didn't know how, like a service you wanted, but then didn't buy. Why did you get stuck? How might your prospective clients get stuck in trying to buy from you? How can you streamline your sales process to make it easier for your clients to buy from you?
- What's not working about your offer? What could you tweak to make it work better? Who could you ask for feedback? What confidence level do you exude? How do your prospects perceive you?
- What could a pivot do for your business? What could a pivot do for your clients? Do you feel like you need permission to pivot your business? What if you had that permission? What do you need for it to be okay to let go of offers in your business that aren't working and explore pivoting?

During the first four steps of the Process of ALLOWING Clarity, the focus has been on designing your business selfishly: allowing your inner light to shine as you focus on what you want, connecting to your true self, identifying and describing your favorite client, and offering to lead them through your signature process to achieve the results they desire.

In Stage 2 of this book, we'll take the insights we've uncovered so far and blend them to craft a message that clearly communicates who you are, what you do, and who you serve.

If you want more support with this chapter's exercises, schedule a free Clarity Call (amandahyoung.com/free). I'll be happy to help you create a signature process so you can offer to lead your clients to achieve the success of their dreams.

Stage 2 –
Communicate Clearly

"Wise men talk because they have something to say;
fools, because they have to say something."
Plato

When you allow clarity to surface in your life and set aside time to uncover what you truly want as you design your business to meet your needs, it becomes much easier to express yourself and ask for what you want.

Stage 2 of this book includes two steps and focuses on clearly communicating who you are, who you serve, what you do, and the results you get for your clients. With the clarity you gained from completing the exercises in Stage 1 (Design Selfishly), you'll apply the insights you've uncovered to speak clearly about your business and create an easy way for the people you meet to provide you with great referrals.

Chapter 7 – Write Your Pitch

"If you can't explain it simply, you don't understand it well enough."
Albert Einstein

ALLO*W*ING – *W* is for *W*rite Your Pitch

If you've ever been to a networking event or any social gathering as an adult, your occupation has come up as a frequent topic of conversation. You'll meet someone for the first time and inevitably the question will be, "So, Jane, what do you do?" As a society, we have learned to value an individual's contribution to our workforce and use their answer to paint a picture of their education, success, financial situation, and social status. It can be a charged question, for many reasons, mostly because we fear how the other person will judge or perceive us based on our answer. As an entrepreneur, this is an often overlooked, and dreaded, opportunity to promote your business.

The fifth step in the Process of ALLOWING Clarity is to Write Your Pitch. To confidently know what to say when someone asks what you do, you need to prepare a response that supports your business. By crafting a simple message that clearly communicates what you do, who you serve, and the results you get, you empower everyone you meet to become part of your marketing team.

When I say, "Write your pitch," that doesn't mean I'm also going to say you need to recite it as a sales pitch to everyone you meet. Your sales process starts with making people aware that your services exist, but instead of pitching your services to everyone you meet, you'll share a little bit about yourself so that they can connect you with people who might benefit from your services. Your pitch is a prepared way to make referrals more likely and to connect with your favorite clients.

Talking about what you do doesn't have to feel dirty or slimy. If you are passionate about what you do, it should feel great to share it with everyone you meet.

Your Elevator Speech

An elevator speech is a short description about what you do that you can say to a stranger in the time it takes to ride in an elevator together for a couple of floors. It needs to be clear, concise, and purposeful. Many people make the mistake of using labels like their job titles to describe their business. When you say, "I'm an attorney," it doesn't paint a picture fast enough and can leave your audience confused. I recently met a parent on the playground who said, "I'm in finance." After asking a few follow-up questions, I discovered he works in the renewable energy sector dealing with solar panels. The company he works with is struggling in the current economic climate, so he might need a career change soon. As a natural networker, and once I knew more, I thought of someone I could connect him with if he needed to make connections for a new job. But he didn't make it easy for me, and someone who isn't a natural networker would more likely have changed the topic soon after he said, "I'm in finance."

A Successful Pitch

To make it easy for the people you meet to understand and take interest in what you do, invite them into a bigger conversation. There are formulas you can use to draft an elevator speech that invites interesting discussions, but they can often come across as being forced. You aren't a robot so don't speak like one or memorize a pitch that sounds so rehearsed it turns people off. The good news is that when you craft an elevator pitch that feels good, you'll deliver it more naturally.

There are six keys to a successful pitch:

Keep it short, but descriptive. Do you want to hear someone talk about their job for less than a minute, or do you want the twenty-minute sales pitch? Most people like talking about themselves more than listening to other people. You aren't telling them your life story, or even selling your services to them. You just want to offer a glimpse into how you spend most of your time and what you're passionate about, to create an opening for additional conversations. When you offer up a short statement about what you do, it should be designed to spark interest and inspire follow-up questions that delve deeper into your work. If you start too vague – "I'm an attorney" – the follow-up questions won't get much beyond the surface, as they're usually about determining what type of attorney and who you work with. If you cover those two topics from the beginning, the follow-up questions can lead to examples of your work, cases you've successfully won, and new strategies your practice is employing to improve the outcomes your clients receive.

Know your audience. When you are surrounded by strangers, it's good to avoid jargon and keep your message simple. But use caution. Don't dumb down your work in a way that can be construed as insulting. Instead, summarize the work you do as concisely as possible or offer an example in layman's terms. Consider removing the word "basically" from your vocabulary, as it can discount your audience's intelligence and be insulting.

If you are in a room full of peers, adjust your pitch to reflect their knowledge level, so that you don't sound obvious or redundant. You can use more jargon and focus more on who you work with and the results you get. If you're a magician at a magic conference, you can differentiate yourself by specifying that you're a corporate magician for Fortune 500 companies, offering a clean act to inspire creative thinking in the next generation of new hires.

Explain who you work with. This is where your target market comes into play. If you have a specific label you can apply to narrow your target, like orthodontists, newlyweds, or celebrity divorce mediators, use it here and elaborate on the problem your target is currently suffering from. Maybe you find qualified assistants for orthodontists, help newlyweds finance their first homes, or offer confidential administrative services for high-profile divorce cases. You can also focus on a specific outcome instead of a specific label, like sleep-deprived parents searching for safe ways to get their newborns to sleep through the night.

Explain the results you get for your clients. You don't need to get technical, but include the services you provide in a way that most people you meet will understand. This is an area with room for creativity. If you have a well-known position that most people you meet will be familiar with, like baker, add specific results to your description. Do you bake loaves of sweet and savory bread to excite discerning palettes? Or do you bake elaborate, themed cakes for memorable birthday parties?

If your job entails a title that is more vague or confusing, like a mentalist or intuitive, offer a brief explanation of the results your clients get and consider leaving out your label altogether to limit confusion. You could also use this situation to educate your audience about your unique career. Conversations can be started by simply stating the outcome you achieve for your clients: I help homeowners restore family heirlooms and artwork after devastating fires.

If you offer multiple services, pick the most popular one or the most relevant service for the audience you are speaking to, and start with that. If you offer commercial and residential carpet cleaning and are at a friend's 40th birthday party, you're likely surrounded by homeowners, so lead with your residential carpet cleaning services and expand into the commercial side if someone seems interested. You can say, "I clean carpets in pet-lovers' households to extend their useful life and keep them looking like new."

Say why your clients work with you. Real estate professionals have it especially rough in their crowded industry when it comes to differentiating themselves. If you're a real estate agent, being able to say why clients work with you is an opportunity to stand out.

Whatever your field, if you have a specialty or can provide insights that prospective clients would likely find valuable, slip them into your pitch. I selected my real estate agent because he had construction experience flipping homes and had the vision for how a home could be transformed. A different real estate agent might have a strategy for selling your home within a week. Others might specialize in working with investment properties, first-time home buyers, short sales, or foreclosures.

Describe symptoms your prospect suffers from. When you elaborate on who you work with by adding specific symptoms they have, your conversation partner will know exactly who they can send to you for help. If you provide tax accounting services for actors and artists, you might describe them as "creative spirits who find no joy in preparing their taxes." By noting a few common complaints your prospects might have, or actions they take, in your conversations, you give the listener the information they need to be on the lookout for prospective clients for you.

Maybe your clients come to you complaining that they hate shopping for clothing whenever the seasons change, and that's what makes them candidates for your personal shopping services. Maybe you help match qualified talent to open positions, and your prospect has fired their third assistant this year because they weren't a good fit. Maybe you're a dog trainer with clients who say, "I wish I could get my dog to stop pulling on her leash every time we go for a walk." You can include these symptoms when talking directly to prospective clients and referral partners alike. The prospective clients will say, "That's me!" or "It sounds like my friend Jan could use your help." Your referral partners will be able to watch for people they meet who exhibit the symptoms of your favorite clients and connect the two of you with a referral. Including the symptoms your clients display can really boost the effectiveness of your pitch with little effort.

Reflection questions: How can you make your pitch short, but descriptive? What are two types of audiences you're likely to encounter? How can your pitch shift to apply to each of those audiences and tell them who you work with, the outcomes you achieve, why your clients work with you, and what your prospects are like?

The Magic Pitch Formula

You'll need to practice your pitch, finesse it as you see how people react to it, and, most importantly, get it to feel right when you say it out loud, so it doesn't sound like a recorded message.

This is the Magic Pitch Formula I use and recommend: "I help (insert your favorite client description) (insert the unique and specific service you provide) so that (insert the benefit, outcome, or result clients realize by working with you)."

For example:

- I help first-time homebuyers navigate the home buying process so that they can rest easy knowing they are getting a home that will support them for years to come.
- I help overwhelmed entrepreneurs clarify their vision for their business so that they can confidently take action toward their goals.
- I help trial lawyers curate a wardrobe of flattering outfits so that they look professional and feel confident in situations ranging from client meetings to courtrooms.

Reflection question: Using the Magic Pitch Formula, what is your pitch?

Confirm Your Pitch

Be sure to test out your pitch with people you know are your target market, to confirm that you are heading in the right direction. Your target market needs to identify with your description of them, and they need to understand and desire the results you are promising. If you call your target market "small business owners," thinking that they will have five to ten employees, you need to be sure that is how they would categorize themselves. If, instead, they think of themselves primarily as "entrepreneurs," "company founders," or "revolutionaries," they might not respond to being called "small business owners".

When you tell people the results you help your clients get, you're planting a seed so that your conversation partner can ask a question about your work, and you can follow up with more detail. This offers you time to explain in more depth how you help clients. The deeper you go in such a conversation, the better a connection you'll make and the higher the likelihood will be of having a new client result from your conversation – either the person you're talking with or someone they refer to you.

For example, if you help your clients feel confident in the courtroom, the person you're talking with might ask you how you do that. Then you can explain a bit of your signature process: how you clean out their closet, teach them what colors and styles work best for their body type, shop with them for key pieces, and show them how to coordinate outfits that are appropriate for work. That can lead to a recent success story where you spoke to a group of new hires at a law firm and were hired to teach them how to shop for a professional wardrobe. Telling that story educates your listener while showing that you talk to large law firms on dressing for success.

Reflection question: Who are some of your favorite clients that you can test your pitch with to see if it resonates?

Start Better Conversations

Make it easy for people to talk to you. Don't be the person at the party or networking event who walks around asking everyone, "So, what do you do?" Instead, try to break the ice and set your conversation companion at ease with a more inviting question.

- What brings you to this event?
- How do you know our host?
- Have you been to this event before?
- Are you a member of this group or a guest?

After they answer, you can respond with your answer and segue into your profession. "This is my first time here. I help therapists attract more clients to their practices and thought this event would be a great place to meet people in the industry." You could then pass the conversation back to them by asking if they work in the industry.

If you're at a more social gathering, you might end up talking about a hobby or how you are connected to the event. If there is a topic that you can connect to your business or a story you can tell about something funny that happened with one of your clients, you open up the conversation to shift into a discussion of your professional lives.

In some cases, you might not discuss your profession the first time you meet someone. That's okay. If they are someone you want to know, have faith that you'll meet them again in good time, or suggest a way to meet again.

It can be helpful before attending social events to set an intention around the people you need to meet coming to you instead of you having to seek them out. When you exude the energy of being grounded and confident in your own space, others will naturally be attracted to that energy and seek you out. I used to think I had to meet as many people as possible to have the best chances of making a quality connection. I've since learned that meeting a few people and having deeper conversations with them is a much better use of my time and far more enjoyable.

Reflection question: What are some interesting questions you can ask to start conversations that put people at ease?

Tell Stories Along the Way

As a child, you may have been told that it isn't nice to talk about how wonderful you are. Being overly self-confident was a bad thing. Maybe you were told not to appear to be too cocky, self-absorbed, arrogant, or conceited. Being a braggart was seen as insulting or impolite. Many of us were taught to dim our inner light in the name of being proper and well-behaved. What a huge mistake!

For entrepreneurs and successful people everywhere, being able to talk about your successes is what gets you more success. When you talk about your passion and shine a light on your gifts, you let others see what gifts you have, what change you can create in the world, and how you can help people; and you exude confidence that attracts more positive energy. When you speak confidently about the work you do, you gain confidence in your abilities and feed your inner light. This is the Law of Attraction: like attracts like. When you shine your light brightly, you allow it to recharge and shine even brighter.

If the idea of talking about yourself and your success has you sheltering your light, it's time to give yourself permission to shine your light. Practice being a successful entrepreneur by speaking confidently about yourself, your gifts, your success, and the results you have helped your clients achieve. If someone you're speaking with doesn't want to hear about how wonderful you are, that's not about you. It's about what they need and it's, therefore, normal and okay for them to drift away from you and your light.

To prepare for talking about yourself, your success, your clients, and your gifts, you can create a couple of stories that are deliberately crafted to support your business by allowing you to talk about what you do. Consider having it be a story that leads you to talk about your passion. Include success stories and show excitement around what you do. This helps to build credibility around your work and heighten your expert status. Remember to use caution when talking about specific clients, especially if you work in an industry where confidentiality is important. Don't use specific names without prior permission and be discrete when necessary.

As I write this chapter, I'm scheduled to attend a networking event as a potential new member of a local group. I intend to introduce myself as someone who helps entrepreneurs get clear on their business so they can move forward with confidence. I'll likely weave in stories about how I'm writing a book to help entrepreneurs design their businesses with heart and passion to achieve their highest level of success. If someone mentions how they aren't getting clients from social media, I can spin that into a story about a personal stylist I worked with who realized she didn't need to spend time or money building up a following on social media, because that wasn't where she gets her clients. If someone talks about how they hate networking events, I can tell them a story about how I helped a client of mine who was really introverted find ways to network that didn't drain all his energy.

I'm not suggesting that you force conversations to focus on what you do or monopolize conversation time with someone you meet. I am suggesting that when someone asks, "What's new?" you can create an opportunity to go deeper into a conversation that allows you to shine your light for someone who might need to see it. And if they don't need to see it, maybe someone they know does.

As mentioned previously, it helps to know your audience. There are times and places where it might not make sense to talk about something great that is happening to you in your business. I was thinking a funeral might be one of those times, but it's just the opposite. Funerals are great times to catch up with people you know, share good things that are happening in your life, and shine some happiness at a time when darkness can be suffocating.

The trick to successfully sharing your stories is to do so from a place of service instead of competition. Share your excitement, love, and happiness with the intention of helping others. Encourage the people you talk with to share about what's going well in their own lives, as well.

Reflection question: What are two success stories you can share about the work you do and the results you have helped your clients achieve?

End with Offering a Favor

Before you end your conversation with someone you've just met, if you have a chance, ask them if there are any connections they are looking for or anyone they want to meet that you might know. They might not have an answer on the spot, but you can offer to help them and exchange contact information so you can follow up if anyone comes to mind later.

Making this offer will likely trigger them to reciprocate. Have your response ready: "I'm always on the lookout for (insert favorite client description) who (insert symptoms your clients have)."

In the next step, we'll go more in depth about how to inspire people to give you referrals and how to expand your referral team. For now, ask for connections to people who work in areas where they are likely to interact with your favorite clients. Maybe they work in a related industry. Maybe they have similar favorite clients, but with a different deliverable. Mortgage brokers often want to meet real estate agents, and divorce attorneys often want to connect with marriage counselors. "A great client for me is (target market) (symptom)."

Reflection question: Who do you want to be introduced to in your business?

Be Consistent

Up to this point, our focus has been on talking about your pitch and what to say when you are speaking directly to someone who doesn't already know about your business. While you are testing out your pitch with people, play around with your language until you get a feel for what works. Once you know what feels right and produces interesting conversations, begin to use that one message consistently throughout your communications, both spoken and written, to establish your branding. You can narrow your pitch down to one line, like advertisers use a tagline, and repurpose it as part of your branding. You might sound like a broken record in your head, but the repetition will secure your position in your industry by creating a memorable description of your services. The confidence that comes with having a smooth and polished pitch will show in your body language and demeanor, and eventually translate into a clear and consistent brand.

When it comes to branding your business, your pitch can be condensed into a short description of what sets you apart. You can boil it down even further to a catchy tagline and use it as a sign-off on training calls, presentations, and videos you create, as well as in your email signature line.

As a professional makeup artist, you might say "I help women put their best face forward when it matters most." The message you would consistently use in your branding would reinforce that by saying, "put your best face forward when it matters most."

As you develop clarity around truly understanding what you want your business to look like, who you want to work with, and what impression you want to make, all the work you have done up until this point contributes to your branding and can be woven throughout the design of all your communications to create a consistent message and theme.

Summary Checklist

To clearly communicate what you do and who you serve, use the following questions to help you write, practice, and polish your pitch:

- How can you make your pitch short, but descriptive?
- What are two audiences you might encounter? How can your pitch shift to appeal specifically to each of those audiences?
- Using the Magic Pitch Formula, write your pitch: "I help (insert your favorite client_description here) (insert the unique and specific service you provide) so that (insert the benefit, outcome, or result clients realize by working with you)."
- Who are some of your favorite clients that you can test your pitch with to see if it resonates?

- What are some interesting questions you can ask to start conversations that put people at ease?
- What are two success stories you can share about the work you do and the results you have helped your clients achieve?
- Who do you want to be introduced to in your business?

Once you've got your pitch drafted and feel like you know how to talk about your business, move on to the next step, where you'll learn about inspiring referrals.

If you want more support around exploring and experimenting with this chapter's exercises, schedule a free Clarity Call (amandahyoung.com/free).

Chapter 8 – Inspire Referrals

"There is only one thing in the world worse than being talked about, and that is not being talked about."
Oscar Wilde

ALLOW*I*NG – *I* is for *I*nspire Referrals

To share your true talents and the amazing results you can help your clients achieve, you need a way for prospective clients to find you. You could advertise and promote your services in a hundred different ways, but the easiest way, and the sixth step in the Process of ALLOWING Clarity, is to Inspire Referrals.

When you are an entrepreneur with limited time to dedicate to marketing, it helps to have a team of people who understand your business, know how to keep a watchful eye open for the clients you are best equipped to serve, trust you, and are willing to recommend your services to people they meet. This doesn't require hiring a team of salespeople. It means teaching the people you know how to refer your favorite clients to you.

Redefining Networking

For most entrepreneurs, traditional networking is an often dreaded, yet necessary, evil of owning one's own business. The good news is it doesn't have to be that way. You can learn to enjoy networking if you expand your definition of networking and become more deliberate about how you network. When you harness your natural tendencies, interests, and abilities, you can discover easier ways to find and attract your favorite clients.

You're bound to fail and despise networking if you think of networking as going to an event with the sole intention of meeting new clients, selling your business to the people you meet, gathering leads, and making small talk in hopes of connecting with someone who can deliver all the favorite clients you need to be successful. If, on the other hand, you honor your personality by attending strategic events to connect with your favorite clients and referral partners on a deeper level, you're more likely to get better results and create a referral network that consistently matches you with outstanding connections and prospective clients who then help you sustain and grow your business. The shift, from dreading networking events that are a waste of time to enjoying networking that gets results, happens when you listen to your inner wisdom, play to your strengths, and find targeted ways to network that match your personality and preferences.

How can you enjoy networking when you hate rooms full of strangers, don't know who to talk to, or aren't a strong conversationalist? You expand your idea of networking to include having coffee with someone you've never met before, sending an email to a former colleague, eating lunch with a friend of a friend, or calling a referral partner to ask what's new and find out how you can help them with their business. Networking doesn't only mean having to attend events that make you uncomfortable around trying to sell yourself to random strangers while they sell themselves to you.

Networking simply means making connections, meeting new people, and maintaining connections with the people you already know. *How* you do that can be personal enough to make it more comfortable for you and thus turn it into a valuable sales tool for your business.

Manage Your Energy

The best way to get good at networking is to create a plan that honors your true self and the way you get your energy. You don't need to step into a room full of strangers if that puts you out of your comfort zone. You could join a small group of entrepreneurs who are also looking for referrals and meet once a month to talk business. By honoring your comfort level and putting yourself in an environment that allows you to relax into your true self, you'll realize far more amazing results and increase your referrals.

To manage your energy, you first need to know if you are an introvert, an extrovert, or a mixture of the two. If you took a personality assessment during the All About You step in the Process of ALLOWING Clarity, you might have been categorized as more introverted or extroverted. Many people confuse introversion with being anti-social and see extroverts as social butterflies who flutter about a room talking to everyone they meet. The definition of introvert or extrovert is actually about how you get energized. People who are more introverted recharge by being alone, while people who are more extroverted receive energy from others.

Understanding your tendencies can guide you to set up meetings and commit to networking opportunities that support your preferences, giving you permission to leave events early when you are drained (if you're an introvert) or attend in-person events when you need to make more direct connections (if you're an extrovert).

Most introverts are easily overstimulated. They are repositories for knowledge, reflective and patient, logical, and internally focused. When speaking with introverts, it's good to note that they dislike being interrupted. If you identify more as an introvert, speed dating and large networking events are not for you. Schedule more intimate meetings and use email and phone conversations to connect with your network.

More extroverted people tend to know a little bit about everything, love variety, enjoy rapid-fire conversation exchanges, move at a fast pace, have a broad focus, and can be seen as more emotional. Extroverts are more externally focused and interested in others.

Understanding the energy tendencies of the people you meet can help you make them more at ease and improve the results of your interactions. If you notice that someone you meet appears more introverted, you might slow down your conversation, find a topic that interests them, and see the interaction as an opportunity to make a deeper connection.

If you have a blend of introverted and extroverted tendencies, even depending on the day, allow yourself flexibility. Maybe this time you want to leave an event early because you're feeling drained. And then you get the idea to throw a party for all your closest friends. Depending on your energy needs, you can limit the number of meetings you take, make time to catch up with friends, or create space for quiet nights at home to replenish your energy.

Listen to your body and what you need to stay energized, alert, and effective when networking.

We live in a predominantly extrovert-centric culture so resources and support for introverts are harder to find, yet there are enlightening ways to deepen your understanding of both personality tendencies. To learn more about introversion, check out Susan Cain's book *Quiet: The Power of Introverts in a World That Can't Stop Talking* and *The Introvert Advantage: How Quiet People Can Thrive in an Extrovert World*, by Marti Olsen Laney Psy. D.

Reflection questions: Do you consider yourself introverted, extroverted, or a combination of the two? What are personality traits you have that support your classification?

Honor Your Self

A client of mine admitted he knew he needed to do more networking to get clients, but he hated it. He was naturally introverted and knew he was an awkward conversationalist. Attending large events had never done much for him in the way of results. All his clients were friends or family or had been referred to him by his clients. The idea of networking didn't have any appeal to him, but he was easy to connect with and passionate about his work once you got to speak with him one-on-one.

Through our work together, he gave himself permission to stop beating himself up for not attending networking events, and he decided to join a local group of small business owners who provided leads to each other. By joining a small group and getting to know its members on a personal level, he was able to make deeper connections, show passion for the work he did, and establish his expertise within the group.

While he made some great connections and got leads on prospective clients, he also allowed himself to change the way he thought about networking to include honoring his introverted tendencies. Instead of being disappointed by repeatedly failing to see results from traditional networking, he found ways to keep in touch with his client base and create referrals by connecting with people in other ways. He wasted less time attending events that made him uncomfortable and invested more time in having one-on-one conversations that supported his needs and his business.

Reflection question: How can you honor your introverted or extroverted tendencies in regard to networking?

Where to Go

The best place to find your favorite clients is wherever they are. To find out where they are, get to know as much about them as you can. If you don't know where they go and what they like to do, ask them, research their interests on Facebook, or survey your favorite clients. Some of them aren't physically going anywhere – they're staying at home. If they are moms of young children, for example, they might be spending twenty minutes a day on Facebook (www.facebook.com). If your favorite clients are job recruiters, you can connect with them at career fairs or online at LinkedIn (www.linkedin.com). Small business owners are attending events held by their local Chamber of Commerce. School board members attend school board meetings and education conferences to learn how to serve their constituents better. When you know where they are, it's easier to get in front of them.

Think of your favorite client. What do you already know about them? Use all the information you gathered from step three in the Process of ALLOWING Clarity – Love Your Clients (Chapter 5) – and consider what organizations they belong to, where they go on a typical day, what they read, what they watch, and how they consume information. Do they read newspapers or industry magazines? Do they watch TED talks or volunteer at their school? Do they take their dogs to the park or spend hours at the gym? Do they commute in the car listening to talk radio, take the train, or work from a home office? Do they follow people or companies online to stay up to date in their industry? The more you know about your favorite clients, their habits, their dreams, and the actions they take, the easier it will be to find them where they are, get your message in front of them, and help them.

In addition to knowing about your favorite clients, know where you are when you're in your element and at your best. Where do you like to go? Where do you spend your time? Is there a space where you overlap with your favorite clients? Do you like attending events and meeting new people, or prefer using your computer as a buffer?

If you tend to be more introverted, you might prefer small gatherings that are less stimulating, like meetings in quiet coffee shops. You might prefer to attend conferences where you already know the topic well, and you might want to consider more venues and opportunities than only the obvious places one learns about your industry. If you have a love of books, you might frequently visit the library or your local bookstore and find your favorite clients there, too. That could lead to an opportunity to host a free introductory weight-loss seminar to a small group at your library to promote your weight-loss coaching.

If you tend to be more extroverted, you might prefer larger and louder conferences with motivational speakers inspiring you from a stage, where you can learn something new and meet new friends. That could lead to an opportunity to take the stage yourself.

Wherever you go, be comfortable. It's okay to leave when you start to feel drained. It's okay to seek out groups if you crave an in-person connection. It's better to spend time doing things that interest you in spaces that support your true self. The thrill of making new connections in ways that suit you fuels your excitement, and you'll shine even brighter.

Reflection questions: Where are your favorite clients? Where are you most comfortable networking?

Who to Meet

As the saying goes, it's not what you know, it's who you know. It doesn't matter if you know a thousand people or a hundred, what matters is the relevance of the people you know. If you have a dog-walking service and know a thousand people with cats, you're out of luck. But if you know a hundred people with dogs that need to be walked when their owners aren't available, you're in business.

Before you step into an event, host a seminar, or consider advertising for clients online, be able to clearly describe what you're looking for. If you were planning to attend a charity fundraiser and needed something to wear, you'd want some clarity about what to look for before you go shopping. Is it going to be a formal event or a casual barbeque? By clarifying and describing what you need from your networking activities, including who you want to meet, you're much more likely to make connections with your favorite clients, or people who can connect you to your favorite clients.

There are four main classifications of people to meet when networking for clients and inspiring referrals: your favorite clients, power partners, industry experts, and connectors.

Favorite Clients. Whenever possible, go directly to the source and meet your favorite clients personally. Going back to the second *L* in the AL*L*OWING process, Love Your Clients, know who your favorite client is and be able to describe them. This will help to put you in situations where you'll be more likely to be introduced to them.

Power Partners. Your power partners work with similar clients as yours and have favorite clients that match your business. One way to find your power partners is that they're people whose services your favorite clients are likely to ask you to recommend. In my case, I work with entrepreneurs who are looking for help marketing their businesses. They often need graphic designers, website developers, virtual assistants, headshot photographers, and bookkeepers to help their businesses run more smoothly. Quality providers of those services are my power partners.

The idea behind power partners is to build trust with one another and refer clients to each other to better serve your clients.

The sequence of events and how your favorite clients make decisions can affect the effectiveness of your power partners. While real estate agents, mortgage lenders, home inspectors, moving companies, and appraisers all work with people who are buying houses, most home buyers start with real estate agents and ask them to recommend other professional services along the way. To be strategic, spend the most time meeting the power partners who interact with your favorite clients before they need your services.

Similarly, the more specialized and focused your partners are, the better. If you plan high-end celebrity weddings, a power partner might be a personal trainer for celebrities. You'll refer your clients to the personal trainer to help with getting into shape for their wedding day, and the trainer will recommend celebrities to you for wedding planning. Because of the timeline of events for a wedding, note that the wedding planner would likely give more referrals to the personal trainer. A wedding planner may get more referrals from a custom engagement ring designer as a power partner because an engagement traditionally happens before a wedding planner is hired.

Industry Experts. People who offer similar services but work with clients you don't serve can be a great source of referrals. By forming partnerships with companies that are bigger or smaller than yours and work with different clients, you can capture what I call the confused prospects. An example of a confused prospect is someone who contacts an architect they know or have heard of because they need an architect. But if that architect only designs high-rise buildings and the prospect wants to have a summer home designed, they're out of luck. The architect can help the confused prospect by referring them to an industry expert who specializes in residential design and who's better able to help with their summer home.

When you become an industry expert and can act as a referral hub – referring prospective clients out to the specialists they need – prospects will keep coming back to you for help. If you're a divorce attorney, you can refer someone who needs a specialist in intellectual property law to someone you know, while also letting them know more about what you do and your specialty, so that, if they meet anyone who needs your services, they will remember and refer you.

Super Connectors. Some people are natural networkers. Their brains are wired to match people who need help to people who can help them. I call them "super connectors." Having a few of them referring business to you can be very helpful. You'll be able to identify super connectors because they will be greeting everyone at an event and know most of them by name. On LinkedIn, they have hundreds of connections in a variety of industries. They are the people who know everyone, and who everyone knows. Super connectors are great people to stay in touch with. Be sure they clearly know what you do, how you are different, who you work with, and who you want to meet, so that they can assign you the proper category in their mental contact database and then connect you with the right prospective clients.

If you're at a new event full of strangers, look for the host or organizer of the event, someone you already know, and anyone who looks like a super connector. If you meet the host, ask for an introduction to someone specific you want to meet. Depending on the event, that could be your favorite clients, your power partners, your industry experts, or a super connector. If you can secure a minute with the guest list before the event or on the way in, scan it for anyone you want to meet so that you can ask the host or someone you know for an introduction.

* * *

If you're networking at an event, what do you do when you get stuck speaking with someone and want to move on? You can excuse yourself to the restroom, let them know you need to get a drink or ask them to help you find someone. Having someone specific you want to meet can be a great way to remove yourself from seemingly less important or interesting conversations during an event. Simply saying, "I'm hoping to meet (insert specific person, power partner, or industry expert) today. Do you know anyone I should talk to here?" You can then show your gratitude to them and move on.

One final tip for figuring out who to meet when you're trying to inspire referrals is to change your energy. Instead of seeking out the people you need to meet and hunting them down in the middle of a crowded room, get clear on who you want to meet and ask the universe to deliver the people you need to meet to you. When you have confidence that you aren't missing out on the opportunity to meet the one person in the room who can change your life and help you reach your dreams, your energy will naturally attract the people you need and make the whole process of networking easier, more fun, and more fruitful.

Reflection questions: What power partners make sense to connect with to provide you with referrals? Do your favorite clients hire another service before hiring you? What other services do your favorite clients need? Who else are they working with that you aren't competing with for business? What industry experts do you need to meet? Who are super connectors you know that you can ask for referrals?

Who Can You Help?

Human tendency, according to Robert B. Cialdini in his book *Influence*, is to "try to repay, in kind, what another person has provided us." He calls this the rule of reciprocation. Marketers understand this rule well and knowingly exploit it. Doing things like offering free samples to get you to buy products or including address label stickers in an envelope requesting a charitable donation leaves people feeling indebted. My point is not to suggest that you manipulate people, but to heighten your awareness of how referrals work – they allow you to be reciprocal, to serve others while serving your own best interests.

Networking is about connecting people for their mutual benefit. To inspire referrals, ask the people you meet how you can help them. Is there anyone they are looking to meet? Do they have a specific type of client you can send their way? Is there a resource you can connect them with to solve a challenge they might be facing? Whenever possible, do something for the favorite clients, power partners, industry experts, connectors, and everyday strangers you meet in life to help others, trigger the rule of reciprocation, and feel good about inspiring referrals. When you send your partners referrals, they will refer clients to you as a way of thanking you for the referrals you have sent them.

What to Say

In the ALLOWING process, we covered *W* for Write Your Pitch. While it's important to have a pitch prepared and to know ways you can talk about your business, when you have the luxury of time, instead of starting with your pitch, focus on connecting with your conversation partner on a deeper level. If you tend to be introverted, find common interests, talk about what you know, and ask open-ended questions. If you tend to be more extroverted, ask questions to learn about a new topic, try not to interrupt, and listen as much as you talk.

Plan to Follow Up

Once you have connected with people to support your business, put a plan in place for staying in touch with them. For friends and family and the people you meet to refer clients to you, they need to remember you. This doesn't mean you send them an email every week or call them daily or weekly to ask for referrals, but it would be good to check in with them each quarter to see how they are doing, what's new in their business, and how you can help them.

When you meet someone new, exchange business cards or contact information and follow up. If you can send them an article that made you think of them, or if you can connect them with someone you know who could help their business, do so. Drop them an email to jog their memory about how you met, reinforce what you do, ask them for what you're looking for, and offer to help them should they be looking for something specific as well. Doing so will create an email trail if they need to refer someone to you later.

There are many ways to stay in touch with your referral partners. Keep a list of contact information handy and include friends, family, and referral partners. Prioritize the list by the likelihood that they will refer clients to you. Then, as part of doing your business, stay in touch with them via social media, email, e-newsletter, mail, or phone. Reach out to your top tier of referral partners quarterly to maintain your most promising relationships.

Reflection question: What's your process for staying in touch with contacts you meet? Who have you received referrals from and how can you continue to receive referrals from them?

Listen

"When people talk, listen completely. Most people never listen."
Ernest Hemingway

One often overlooked key to inspiring referrals is to simply be present during conversations and listen. If you want others to listen to what you have to say and to help you, listen to what they have to say and offer to help them. Participate actively in the conversation and make it a point to learn their name. If you are someone who tends to be bad at remembering names, consider reading Joshua Foer's book, *Moonwalking with Einstein,* for great tips on how to improve your memory.

You can take listening one step further by making notes about the people you meet so that you have a way to reconnect with them the next time your paths cross. If, when you first met them, they mentioned seeing a great concert, on your next encounter you can ask if they have been to any good concerts recently. It shows that you listen, care, and take a genuine interest in them as a person.

By connecting more deeply with people you meet throughout your life, you'll become more memorable, more likable, and more trustworthy. As a result, you'll easily inspire referrals.

Summary Checklist

The more you train the people you meet to understand what you do, who you serve, and how to identify a good referral for you, the more referrals you'll receive. To inspire referrals, honor your tendencies, and become a more effective networker, answer these questions:

- Do you consider yourself introverted, extroverted, or a combination of the two? What are personality traits you have that support your classification? How can you honor your introverted or extroverted tendencies regarding networking?

- Where are your favorite clients? Where are you most comfortable networking?
- What power partners make sense to connect with to provide you with referrals? Do your favorite clients hire another service before hiring you? What other services do your favorite clients need? Who else are they working with that you aren't competing with for business? What industry experts do you need to meet? Who are super connectors you know that you can ask for referrals?
- What's your process for staying in touch with contacts you meet? Who have you received referrals from and how can you continue to receive referrals from them?

Over time, your referral network will grow and you'll receive more referrals from people you meet and your satisfied clients. Use the Process of ALLOWING Clarity to Inspire Referrals and network in ways that honor your true self and support your business.

Now that you understand how to inspire referrals in your business, move on to Stage 3 and get ready to Act Imperfectly.

If you want more support around exploring and experimenting with this chapter's exercises, schedule a free Clarity Call (amandahyoung.com/free).

Stage 3 – Act Imperfectly

"Imperfect action is better than perfect inaction."
Harry S. Truman

After designing your business selfishly and crafting your message to communicate clearly, you're now ready to act imperfectly. As entrepreneurs, we want to do things well. We are competitive and take pride in the work we do, but our perfectionist tendencies can paralyze us, keeping us from taking the necessary steps to realize our success. I'm not suggesting you slop things together, cut corners, or carelessly blast through your work just to check stuff off your task list. Take deliberate and focused action to get things done. Stop making excuses and delaying your success until everything is just right and start serving your favorite clients.

If you're waiting for permission to do something, give yourself permission to do it now. If you're waiting for things to be ready, allow space for them to be ready now. If you're scared, give your fear a seat in the co-pilot's chair and take the very next step toward your success now.

Nike says it best: "Just do it."

Chapter 9 – Notice Your Needs

"Happiness is the settling of the soul into its most appropriate spot."
Aristotle

ALLOWI*N*G – *N* is for *N*otice Your Needs

Starting your own business isn't something you do alone. You might feel like since you're a smart person you should be able to figure out how to create a successful business by yourself, but it isn't always that simple. Having a successful business means being able to get all the right pieces in place to provide a quality service to the right people, and being able to ask for, and invest in, help. It takes planning and a broad understanding of business and marketing concepts that don't always show up as natural talents. We know we want to serve people and be our own boss but making that declaration and setting that intention doesn't give us the tools and knowledge we need to run a successful business, no matter what degrees we've earned.

The generic advice and broad ideas spewed by articles professing the benefits of entrepreneurship are great for getting you inspired and pointing you in the right direction, but when it comes to building a sustainable business, you're going to need help along the way.

While many entrepreneurs take pride in bootstrapping their businesses and doing it alone, they also invest a lot of their time, energy, and resources trying to find the answers they need to get and keep their businesses on track. Many of them fail because this wasn't meant to be a solo gig.

To identify what it takes to start a successful business without wasting valuable time and get the support you need, follow this step in the Process of ALLOWING Clarity and Notice Your Needs.

What Do You Need?

Even though I knew I wanted to be an entrepreneur decades ago, I didn't know how. I thought I could read books about entrepreneurship, study magazine articles detailing the steps to take, earn a business degree (or two), and magically I would be an overnight business success, taking sweet vacations and driving fancy cars. But when the time came for me to dip my toe in the water and create my own business, I realized that I didn't know how to stay afloat, let alone swim.

The missing piece of my plan was having a mentor – a business coach or guide with the experience of having gone before me on this new path I was embarking upon to let me know where the pitfalls were and how to navigate through the challenges that presented themselves.

Up until that point in my life, my parents had guided me through most of my decisions. My friends were there for me when I needed relationship and fashion advice.

And, once I got married, my husband became a voice of reason and insight and helped me make important life decisions. But when it came to owning my own business, my parents, my husband, nor my friends could support or advise me to make the right decisions – because they hadn't traveled the path I was traversing.

It would have been like calling my dad from Paris and asking him where to go for a late-night snack since my jet-lagged body had slept straight through dinner. He had never been to Paris, didn't know the language, and had no idea what restaurants were open at that time of night. When I asked my tour guide, who knew Paris and all the best sites to see, and restaurants for experiencing true French culture, I got the expert advice I needed.

To reach your business goals, find the people qualified to lead you. Your friends and family aren't always qualified for the job no matter how desperately they want to help you. They often want to help so badly and fear leading you down the wrong path, that they get what I call Bobble-Head Syndrome, where they just smile and nod at whatever you say. They don't question why you're taking the actions you're taking, or they ask too many questions and leave you feeling even more hopeless and confused. They can't help you think through your challenges from a strategic standpoint because they haven't been in your situation and don't have the answers. Each of them has their role to play in your life, but the role of business advisor, mentor, or coach isn't likely to be filled by the people you're closest to.

To make matters worse, as entrepreneurs we tend to be fast thinkers who have more ideas than we know what to do with. We're easily distracted, lured down rabbit holes without even knowing how we got down there. When you surround yourself with mentors, experts, and advisors who understand where you're going and what you're trying to achieve, you can avoid the pitfalls and common distractions that delay most entrepreneurs.

Reflection questions: Who are the people you're closest to in your life and what roles do they play to support you? Who are the experts in your life who can tell you when you're going off on a tangent and need to get back on track? Who can help you strategically think through your challenges and avoid common pitfalls in your business?

Satisfy Your Needs

While attending a party at a neighbor's home, the topic of promoting talented workers into management positions came up. We discussed a concept from one of my favorite books, *First, Break All the Rules*, by Marcus Buckingham and Curt Coffman. The main advice is that corporations shouldn't promote their best people into management positions just because they want to honor their achievements by moving their star employees up a corporate ladder. Instead, they need to find creative ways to acknowledge their employees' talents and support their growth in ways that don't include promoting them away from positions where they thrive. Thinking that all good workers will make good managers is a dangerous assumption. Similarly, thinking that you, as an entrepreneur, are good at everything, is an equally dangerous assumption. You might be able to wear many hats, but that doesn't mean they all look good on you.

The truth is that we all have our true talents, and we all have areas where our capabilities fall short. The key to success in your business, in your career, and in the rest of your life is to spend as much time using your true talents and doing things that bring you joy.

To design a business you enjoy and a life you desire, find ways to satisfy your needs. Know what brings you joy and how to delegate the tasks that don't. This might not be something you can achieve as an entrepreneur who's just getting started, but it's something you can aspire to by identifying the ways you can spend time doing what you love and delegating what you can.

Value Your Time

When you're just starting out in your business and money is tight, you might think that you're making the right decisions by designing your logo, building your website, and doing your bookkeeping. If those skills fall under your true talents, then they do make sense for you to do yourself. But if they aren't your true talents, it's better to invest in the *results* you want than investing time, money, and energy trying to learn new skills that won't serve you or the long-term goals of your business.

The Law of Diminishing Returns is the point at which the results we get become less valuable than the resources used to achieve them. As an entrepreneur, hours spent doing work that doesn't fall within your umbrella of true talents is less productive and ends up costing you more in your business in the long run. If you could be investing your time in generating income by working directly with your clients or promoting your business to attract new clients, but instead spend your time trying to figure out how to design your website, then your website is costing you more than it would be if you outsourced it to someone whose true talent is designing websites. Why take 20 hours to do something someone else can do in five hours while you can invest your 20 hours into something you're better at doing? When you focus on doing what you're best at, you'll attract the income needed to invest in the results you really want.

It might sound appealing to save money by figuring things out on your own, but the risk you run in doing everything yourself is doing things wrong and thus delaying your success even more. If you truly have no talent for creating websites or designing logos, find a way to get the support you need to get them done – or do without those pieces of your business until they're absolutely necessary and you are ready to invest in them.

If you need more time to work on your business, consider ways to lighten your workload in other areas of your life besides your business – like hiring a housekeeper or babysitter – and invest in the success of your business.

Reflection questions: What areas do you need to invest in to achieve the results you want in your business? What actions do you need to take to make those investments? Are those actions revenue-generating? Are they necessary? Do they serve you well? What can you delegate from your to-do list? What can you eliminate? What roles and tasks in your business bring you joy? What roles and tasks do you want to continue doing?

Beware of Free Advice

A friend on social media posted a comment about needing a title for her latest book and asked a large group of friends to chime in. As they were voting, rewording her title, and crafting a subtitle that fit together nicely, I was the contrarian voice in the thread. My advice to her was to sift through the feedback and, instead of taking the popular vote for her final title, take a step back and reconnect to the purpose of her book. Asking a wide range of friends with various backgrounds who weren't necessarily her target market and didn't even know what the book was about, wasn't going to get her a great title. She needed to reconnect with her purpose and her audience, then sift through all the ideas she'd gathered and *then* string them together into something beautiful that captured the essence of what she was trying to communicate.

While it's great to gather insights from many sources, it's even more important to have someone on your team who can help you sift through your work to find the gems and string them together when you are so deeply engrossed in what you're doing that you can't tell the rocks from the rubies; someone who understands your unique situation, knows how to match your talents with your audience, and can help you craft your message in a way that your clients can hear and be inspired by. Free advice can be a great place to start, but if you don't connect it back to your goals, make sure it matches your capabilities, and know how it will connect with your favorite clients, it can do more harm than good.

I hear entrepreneurs constantly wondering if they should be using the latest social media platform, investing in advertising, or attending more networking events. My advice to all of them is to reflect on the bigger picture of their businesses and see how each opportunity they encounter connects to their overall goals.

As a marketing strategist, even I seek help with my marketing and messaging, because I'm too close to the work I'm doing. We don't know what we don't know, and we can't always see what's right in front of us. I find that I perform best when I have a business coach helping me filter my ideas and stay in alignment with my goals.

Be Accountable

When you're your own boss, you make the rules and oversee how you spend your time. The freedom of entrepreneurship can often breed indecision in the form of distraction and procrastination. It can produce busyness that only *appears* to be productive but is avoidance in disguise.

To make the most use of your time and reach your goals, notice how you spend your time and how that relates to the results you're achieving. When we aren't clear around our actions and are unsure of what we need to be doing to advance our work and serve our clients, we often hide behind tasks that make us feel like we are being productive when we are actually hiding from the fact that we aren't sure what we need to be doing. By clearly identifying the steps you need to take each day or week in your business, you'll be able to track your progress and maintain focus on your destination.

Simply noticing that you need help staying on task and focusing on the clients you serve can be incredibly beneficial to your business. Enlist a friend to serve as an accountability partner – someone to help hold you accountable to the tasks you want to achieve each week, while you do the same for them. Depending on how much help you need and how often, you can design a weekly or monthly check-in system with your partner to stay focused and continue moving toward your goals in your business. Limiting your check-in calls or emails to task items you need to accomplish will keep your accountability system supportive instead of providing an additional distraction. Structure your partnership to support both your business and your accountability partner's. And remember to celebrate every win – from landing a new client and achieving revenue goals to saying no to an opportunity that wasn't a good fit or releasing a difficult client.

Reflection questions: Who can you partner with to help you stay accountable to your business? How often do you need to connect? What boundaries can you set to keep your accountability partnership supportive?

Consider a Coach

Navigating the path of entrepreneurship alone can be challenging and lonely. Before I found my first business coach online, I had no idea there even was such a job title, let alone what they did or who they served. I originally thought I had to already have a successful business to have a business coach, but I quickly learned that wasn't the case.

My first business coach helped me understand the steps I needed to launch my business and attract my first clients. Working with her gave me access to a wealth of entrepreneurs like me who were in the same situation and struggling with the same issues. I had a framework to follow that helped me focus my time, and I had a resource to reach out to whenever I was struggling to find answers. I learned the value of being coached as part of a group, where I connected with others while learning from the situations they face and the questions they asked and answered. And I learned the power of individual coaching to provide customized solutions that were unique to my individual needs.

Beyond all the knowledge, clarity, and confidence I've gained from working with various coaches, I've found it most helpful that my coaches have been able to see my situation from a different vantage point and reflect my ideas in a way I could understand even better. I call this the Outsider Effect. An expert outsider looking in can help you become a truly inspiring leader in your business.

Join a Community

Have you ever walked into a space, looked around the room, and realized you were surrounded by people with common interests who understood you from the moment you arrived? That's the feeling I got when I attended my first event with my business coach. I suddenly found myself surrounded by women who were in the same situation, facing similar struggles, with a desire to make a difference in the world by offering their services and knowledge to help others. It was magical. I had finally found my happy place, where I could be myself, speak my mind, and be supported for who I was.

With so many different organizations and groups available to entrepreneurs, it can be a challenge to find a community that will embrace you for who you are and make you feel welcome and supported. But it makes such a big difference to your journey.

It doesn't have to be a homogeneous group, just one with common values and people you connect with. It helps if the group has a leader or role models with successes you can aspire to and stories you can learn from. They might have similar customers or be in a similar industry as you, but they need to be diverse enough for you to gather new ideas and gain new perspectives to take back and apply to your work. Above all, they need to provide a safe space in which you can be yourself, be vulnerable, and get the support you need to thrive.

Reflection questions: Who do you need to be surrounded with to feel safe and supported? What community can you join to help your business thrive?

Summary Checklist

By setting aside time to notice your needs and focus on how you can be supported in your business, you'll find yourself reaching your goals and realizing your success much more quickly. To notice your needs, answer the questions and complete the exercises listed below:

- Who are the people you're closest to in your life and what roles do they play to support you? Who are the experts in your life who can tell you when you're going off on a tangent and need to get back on track? Who can help you strategically think through your challenges and avoid common pitfalls in your business?
- What areas do you need to invest in to achieve the results you want in your business? What actions do you need to take to make those investments? Are those actions revenue-generating? Are they necessary? Do they serve you well?
- What can you delegate from your to-do list? What can you eliminate? What roles and tasks in your business bring you joy? What roles and tasks do you want to continue doing?
- Who can you partner with to help you stay accountable to your business? How often do you need to connect? What boundaries can you set to keep your accountability partnership supportive?

- Who do you need to be surrounded with to feel safe and supported? What community can you join to help your business thrive?

When you allow yourself to ask for and receive the help you need to create a successful business, you're on the fast track to achieving your goals. As you feel more clear about how to Notice Your Needs and invest in the results you want to realize, move on to the final step where you'll Go! Take Action!

If you want more support around exploring and experimenting with this chapter's exercises, schedule a free Clarity Call (amandahyoung.com/free).

Chapter 10 – Go! Take Action!

"If at first you do not succeed – try to hide your astonishment."
Harry F Banks

ALLOWIN*G* – *G* is for *Go!* Take Action!

Once you're clear on where you want to go, it's time to embark on your journey. You can wait until you're fully ready, but the reality is that you will never be fully ready for anything you do in life. That's part of the journey. We figure things out and learn along the way.

The good news is that, even if you don't feel ready to jump into the deep end just yet, you can start by wading into the shallow end to get a feel for the water one step at a time.

The final step in the Process of ALLOWING Clarity is to Go! Take Action! But don't take any action just to look like you're doing something. Take deliberate, thoughtful actions that meaningfully advance you. To do that, slow down, step back, and look at the specific steps you're taking and why.

Stop Being "Busy"

Our society values being busy. Busyness has evolved as a highly desired trait and an indicator of success. It has become attached to our innate worth and personal sense of accomplishment. We want to appear busy so that we feel like we are contributing to society and doing our part.

As entrepreneurs, we might be busy responding to emails, catching up on social media, attending meetings, making phone calls, and writing reports. Being busy can feel awful. When we're busy, we tend to be overwhelmed, forgetful, confused, distracted, and function at a lower level. Our bodies and minds need time and space to reset, refresh, and regroup. When we're too busy to listen to a friend or our children and are rushing to the next item on our agenda, we aren't living in the moment but chasing after the future. All to feel like we're doing what we think is right and expected of us.

When someone asks, "How are you?" we often respond with "Good. Busy!" or "Busy, but I'm not complaining!" or, as my mom says, "Busy, and out of trouble!" Being exposed to those automatic declarations set the stage for me to believe that being busy was a good thing because it meant I was important and making a difference in the world. Of course, I wanted to be busy! I wanted to be a valued member of society. But I've learned the greater benefits of embracing the opposite, resisting the norm, and being happy instead.

By peeling back our language and the characteristics we value, we can see into our core values and the belief systems that form the foundation for our actions. Some of these beliefs may be limiting us on a subconscious level and holding us back in our business.

When you slow down enough to realize that you have negative beliefs around making money, deserving success, or being enough just as you are, you can begin to shift your beliefs toward ones that are more supportive of your success.

You might think that work has to be hard, money has to be earned, and success doesn't come easily. But what might happen if you shift your thinking and start to believe that serving others is fun, money is easy to attract, and success comes easily? When you trade the beliefs that keep you busy for busyness' sake for beliefs that feel better, you open yourself up to achieve the life of your dreams.

When I delved deeper into my reasons for wanting to associate myself with being busy, I learned that my motivation was to feel valuable, be seen as productive, and accomplish tasks quickly. Imagine my surprise when I realized that I didn't need to complete everything I started!

Then I considered the possibility that going slower would be better in some ways. I found examples to support my new theory and discovered that sometimes doing things slowly produced much better results. That opened a lot of free time in my schedule to do more of what matters most to me. I shifted my belief from being busy and productive to being deliberate and thoughtful.

These small shifts can create big changes in your life. Start by taking your original belief and swapping it out for a better belief. "Doing things quickly is best" becomes, "I take the time I need to do things well."

Reflection questions: Why do you tell people you are busy? Is there a more clear answer you can offer in small-talk situations? What would it feel like to be balanced, excited, or happy instead of busy? How can you be less busy and more deliberate in your actions? What beliefs do you need to change and how can you reframe them?

Maintain Focus

I used to be a multitasking maven. I thought it was a life skill that made me amazingly talented and valuable as an employee, and more qualified to be labeled a "good mom." Instead, I learned that I made more mistakes, forgot to get things done, and wasn't always present when my kids needed me. My attention was so scattered that I was easily agitated and quick-tempered. I still struggle to single-task and frequently fail as I knit while watching television, listen to an audiobook while emptying the dishwasher, and think about my to-do list while writing blog posts.

Scientific studies show that by focusing on one task at a time you can accomplish your work more quickly, with better results. Multitasking causes us to divide our attention and lose valuable momentum as we try to pick up where we left off. While some people might be good at walking and chewing gum while texting on their cell phone, that doesn't mean that's what they should do. With so many distractions vying for our attention at any given moment, it can be challenging to stay focused on anything for an extended period.

As entrepreneurs juggling so many tasks, we frequently fall into the habit of multitasking as our only hope of getting enough done to feel like we are staying afloat.

Establish systems and habits. Instead of running around like a chicken with its head cut off, create systems and establish habits to help you focus on what needs to be done. Instead of having deductible receipts strewn all over your office, keep expense envelopes in your car, in your purse, on your desk, and a folder in your computer to capture your expenses. Then create a habit of collecting them for your bookkeeper or entering them into your financial software each month. By creating a flow for frequent processes and automating as many of your tasks as possible, you'll be less busy in your business and more free to have fun with your work.

Habits can evolve from a problem you identify and create a solution around. In my case, I hate paying late fees for library books. I know the books are due three weeks after I check them out, so I created a habit. I schedule a time to visit the library every three weeks. That appointment on my calendar triggers me to renew the books before their due date if we need to reschedule our library visit.

Let go. If you have too much to do and can't get it all done, let some of it go. You can imagine some of the things you'd have to give up or push off until another time if you had to take time off for an illness or family emergency. If things can wait, let them wait. This might also mean that you say no to various requests and opportunities that aren't important to you. Give yourself permission to say no unless something will truly bring you joy. Fill your days with all things you want to do or absolutely need to do.

Delegate. If you have too much to do, delegate your workload or accept that it won't all get done and let go of the things that aren't important. Repeating tasks are great to delegate because you can teach someone to do them once and have them repeat the task on a set schedule. Sending new client welcome packets, scheduling appointments, creating email newsletters, and entering business expenses can all be delegated tasks. Using virtual assistants is a great way to get help doing tasks you aren't good at or don't enjoy doing.

Beware of excuses you might make around delegating work to someone else. You might want to control everything or think it will take longer to have someone else do the work than for you to just do it. The key to delegating is to delegate the right tasks and communicate your needs clearly. Start small and invest the time to learn from the beginning how to delegate well to save time and reduce headaches in the future.

Prioritize. You can start prioritizing your workload by dumping everything from your head onto paper and sorting it into tasks that are important, not important, urgent, and not urgent. Highlight the items that are revenue-generating so that you can stay focused on attracting money to your business instead of keeping yourself busy on tasks that aren't important or timely. If you sort your tasks into four quadrants, with important and not important tasks on the left side, urgent and not urgent tasks across the top, you'll quickly see that what you need to prioritize will land in the important and urgent quadrant in the upper left-hand corner. Schedule time on your calendar to address those urgent and important priorities each day without question.

Create a holding pen for overflow ideas. If you are overwhelmed by ideas you don't have time for right now, find a place to store them until you are ready for them. You can add to and review them quarterly and thus clear your mind from trying to hold on to every good idea you get. I do this in Evernote software (www.evernote.com) on a note I've named "parking lot" that's linked to my phone, so I can add ideas on the go. I also have a notebook dedicated to creative ideas I'm not ready to execute. Be sure to schedule time on your calendar to review your ideas on a quarterly or annual basis for inspiration.

Create a "waiting for" list. When you need to request something from another person, add it to an ongoing list of items you are waiting for others to complete before you can take action yourself. If you've called the dentist to transfer your medical records, add that to your "waiting for" list as a reminder that it is an open task that needs to be revisited. Whenever I order a gift online or am waiting for someone to send me an important file, I add that item to my "waiting for" list and review it weekly to trigger my next action and limit the number of open tasks my brain needs to manage.

Reflection questions: What habits can you create to make your life run more smoothly? What tasks do you need to let go of? What can you delegate? What tasks are urgent and important? Where can you store your overflow of good ideas? Where can you keep track of open tasks until they are completed?

Plan Your Day

Different organizational strategies work for different people, of course, so figure out what works for you. Do you schedule everything on a paper calendar? Or do you prefer a calendar on your phone? Do you keep notes in a journal? Or stash everything in a sortable software program like Evernote?

If you have tried to get organized and failed repeatedly, don't give up. Look for elements of what does and doesn't work for staying organized. Use techniques you prefer and consider blending a few different methods to customize a routine that supports your business and helps you move toward your goals.

I use a blended method that includes a physical calendar (Moleskine Weekly Notebook) and an online calendar linked to my email (www.google.com/calendar). The online calendar links to an online booking system (www.youcanbook.me) so that clients can schedule appointments easily and see times when I'm available. By linking my calendars together, I can automate appointment scheduling in a way that frees up time for other important and urgent tasks.

To stay organized, I've adopted a weekly practice where I invest thirty minutes a week in reviewing and listing out what I've accomplished, what I haven't completed, challenges I'm facing, solutions to those challenges, and the top five things I want to accomplish in the coming week to feel good about how I've spent my time. I move the five tasks I want to accomplish next to my calendar and prioritize them. This simple practice has helped me maintain focus and stay organized while celebrating my accomplishments. It also provides a record of what I've completed, while shining a spotlight on issues that I'm facing. This way, I attend to them regularly instead of ignoring them and allowing them to snowball into bigger issues.

For this weekly practice to succeed, it's important to allow it to unfold in a way that supports you best. Plan your day by matching times that you're most productive with the work you most need to get done. Match your tasks to your energy availability. If you like working out at lunch and writing in the mornings, block off time on your calendar accordingly.

When you don't get everything done on your list, avoid the urge to judge yourself and instead look at possible explanations as to why you didn't achieve your goals and how you can improve. It's the constant willingness to improve and tweak your process that will lead you to success.

Reflection questions: What system can you create to support your calendar and plan your week? When do you do your best work? How can you match your energy to the tasks you most want to accomplish?

Set Distractions Aside

When I decided to write a book in less than three months, I wasn't sure how it was going to be possible. I started out writing a chapter in three days and ended up drafting each chapter for this book in under four hours simply by getting clear about my purpose, what key points I needed to include, planning what I needed to include where, and then throwing together a draft of my thoughts that was riddled with grammatical errors. By allowing my ideas to flow freely, I was able to quickly capture my thoughts on paper.

Then I went back to each chapter and edited the pages one step at a time with a sharp focus and no distractions. I shut down my email alerts, set my phone to airplane mode, and hid in a quiet room at home. By creating an environment that was free of distractions, I was able to focus all my energy on the task at hand and became more efficient and productive than ever before.

I attribute my success at keeping on task to the Pomodoro Technique (www.pomodorotechnique.com). Its main idea is to set a timer for 25 minutes and set an intention for what you want to get done during that time. When the timer goes off, you take a five-minute break to check email, grab a snack, or stretch your body while resetting your mind. Then you set a new intention for the next 25 minutes and repeat the process until your project, or your workday, is complete. It may seem like an intense way to stay focused, and you might think that you can't make yourself unavailable for 25 minutes at a time, but I encourage you to find a way to test it out and see how it can fit into your daily schedule and boost your productivity.

Some distractions can hold a message for you. If you are avoiding a task and find yourself hiding from your work, ask yourself why. We often avoid a task when we aren't clear enough about it or something doesn't feel right. By connecting with your feelings, you gain a deeper understanding of what's going on and can address the underlying issues.

As I wrote this book, I took imperfect action and organized my thoughts by following my own Process of ALLOWING Clarity to ensure that the message I was writing was the message that would resonate with my favorite clients to help them get more clear in their businesses. I limited distractions and realized that the urge to do something other than the task at hand was a sign that I wasn't clear enough about what I wanted to say or that there was some other emotion at play blocking me from accomplishing my goals. When I took a moment to address those feelings, concerns, or fears, I was able to more easily refocus my efforts and get back on task.

Reflection question: How can you limit distractions in your business?

Take the Right Actions

Because we receive so much advice about how to run a business successfully, it can be difficult to cut through the clutter and resist the temptation of magic solutions. You can cut to the chase and identify the next action steps you need to take to produce results by knowing where you're going.

I often see entrepreneurs beating themselves up for not posting on social media enough or attending networking events, even when those tactics won't necessarily provide them the results they desire. They think having an office or an assistant will solve their business problems, but if they don't have enough business to support an office or enough work for an assistant, they have just created more problems and added to their stress.

The key is to step back and ask yourself if the method you are using will get your desired result. Know why you want a thousand "likes" on your Facebook page. If you aren't sure, you're better off investing in the expert advice you need to get clear around what will and won't work rather than wasting precious time, money, and resources on what I call that the Spaghetti Method: throwing every idea you have at a problem to see what sticks. While that might seem like an action step that's moving you toward your goals, it's not. You'll likely learn a lot, but those will be lessons in what not to do in a successful business.

Reflection questions: How will the tactics you are using get you the results you want? How will your tactics and results work together to support each other?

Release the Shoulds

If you think you *should* be spending more time marketing your business on social media, I encourage you to reflect on why that may or may not work for you. If you think you *should* be sending out a direct mail postcard to instantly attract clients with a cheap offer, you need to know that direct mail has a track record for low response rates and slow results. People might start paying attention after the tenth postcard they receive with your powerful message, but unless you have a close relationship with them through other avenues, it's not the best tactic for you to try. On the other hand, if your prospective clients get your email newsletter, interact with you on Facebook, and then receive a postcard for an upcoming event in their city, your results will likely be much different and more supportive of your goals.

Instead of blindly doing what you think you *should* be doing or what is working for other people, consider your business unique. Your resources and goals might be better served by other techniques.

Being successful isn't about having a beautiful website and the best software to support your business. It's about serving your clients and attracting income to grow your business in a way that expands your reach to more people who can benefit from your services. Don't invest in the wrong tactics that you don't need. Invest in solutions that are likely to work for you and match them to your goals and your comfort level. Invest in actionable solutions as part of a bigger plan to advance your business overall. Avoid taking action on autopilot and start making deliberate choices to design the business you love.

Take Imperfect Action

When things don't go as planned, it's time to take a moment to learn from your mistakes.

Starting out in my business, I feared failure more than anything else. Heeding the advice of the business coaches I met, I learned to take imperfect action and released my perfectionism. It was the mistakes I made and the failure I experienced along the way that taught me the most in my business.

When Sara Blakely, the inventor of Spanx shapewear, was growing up, her father would often ask her the same question at dinnertime. "What have you failed at this week?" She learned that failure wasn't something to be ashamed of but something to embrace as a lesson learned.

Set your ego aside and allow failure to show you a better way to reach your clients, provide great service, and run your business more smoothly.

Generate Revenue

Money issues are rampant among business owners. Depending on the industry you are in, you might think that you shouldn't make money off your clients, or that they don't have enough money to work with you. All the unhelpful stories you tell yourself about money are going to have to be left behind to allow success in your business.

In my three years of working with coaches, I have learned that our mindsets are the most limiting factor in our businesses. I strongly believe in the Law of Attraction, that like attracts like, and have used it to manifest the home office I'm sitting in to write this book. Thoughts become things. You need positive thoughts to see positive results in your life and your business.

Instead of using forceful words like spend, sell, and make money, I've switched to more flowing words like invest, offer, and attract. The energy of these words makes me feel like I'm inviting money and success into my life instead of chasing after it.

If your dog got off his leash, would it be easier to *chase* him down the street or *offer* him a treat to get him to come back to you? All my life, I have been a "go-getter," thinking that more actions would result in more success. What I've learned is that less action that's more deliberate is more effective. By allowing success to come to me, allowing clients to find me, offering to serve clients in a bigger way, and allowing them to invest in their results through me, I've been able to create a business I enjoy.

When you have a service people want, one that provides solutions to their problems and creates the results they want to see in their lives, you offer something valuable. You can honor your gifts and yourself by *attracting* money to your business and *allowing* your clients to happily pay you.

Oftentimes, we fear the entire subject of money in such a way that we don't want to discuss it or deal with it and so we hide behind other parts of our business and ignore our finances altogether. We fidget with the website or rewrite our bio instead of making offers and investing in targeted advertisements to attract prospective clients.

You can choose to hide behind the busy work of your business, or you can choose to prioritize tasks that will attract money to your business. Creating an elaborate website might make you feel like you have a legitimate business, but maybe you could sidestep the money and time that goes into designing and building a formal website and still get the same, or even better, results. Creating a website with a single webpage that captures email addresses or gives your prospects one clear action step to take, might save money and time while focusing your message and achieving better results from your services. This is about working smarter, not harder.

You can buck societal expectations and entrepreneurial norms, skipping traditional methods that don't affect your bottom line and, instead, create a smarter business that gets results that are better for you.

Designing your business is like buying a car. You don't buy a new car before taking it for a test drive to see if you like it and what model you want. Test drive your business to see what features you like and what you want to change before diving headfirst into the deep end with big investments in time and money. When you clearly know what you want, have consistent revenue, and a viable, successful business, then you can invest in polishing your brand, enhancing your website, and adding the bells and whistles that support your business and improve how you serve your clients.

Reflection questions: What steps can you take to directly generate revenue in your business? Will that action alone generate revenue or is it part of several steps needed to attract clients?

Make a Plan

When you understand which methods make the most sense to move you toward your goals, you can align them with your preferred marketing tactics. If you hate social media but love speaking, you can build your business around speaking events that attract clients. If you don't have a lot of money to invest, you can find creative ways to reach your prospective clients through referral networks. If you aren't great at designing marketing plans and figuring out how to reach your goals, invest in the support you need instead of wandering around aimlessly and struggling to figure it out on your own.

When you match the goals you're trying to achieve with the resources you have available and factor your preferences into the mix, you can create a business you love.

Reflection questions: Where are you headed? How will you get there? How do your personal preferences and true talents influence or support your plan? Do you need to invest in help with creating a clear plan?

Visualize Your Success

What does your success look like? How does it feel? How many clients are you serving? What results are they achieving? How many hours are you working? How much money are you attracting? When you get clear about what you want, who you want to work with, how you want to serve them, what you'll say to inspire them, how you can partner with others, and what support you need in your business, your actions will be more effortless, effective, and impactful. You'll see results faster and enjoy having a business that is easier to sustain and you'll be fulfilled by your work.

Paint a vivid picture in your mind, sketch it on paper, describe it in your journal, or create a simple vision board to connect your image of success to the feelings you'll have once you've achieved your goals. Revisit your image and the feelings it evokes as often as possible to connect with your outcome and allow it to manifest in your life. Then watch as it unfolds.

Reflection questions: What does your success look like? How does it feel? How many clients are you serving? What results are they achieving? How many hours are you working? How much money are you attracting? How can you create an image of your success and frequently connect with the feeling it evokes?

Summary Checklist

To work smarter in your business, save time, money, and resources, and be deliberate in the actions you take, create a clear vision of your destination. Along your journey, check in with your vision to be sure that each action you take connects to and supports your vision. Answer the questions and complete the exercises below to Go! Take Action!:

- Why do you tell people you are busy? Is there a more clear answer you can offer in small-talk situations? What would it feel like to be balanced, excited, or happy instead of busy? How can you be less busy and more deliberate in your actions? What beliefs do you need to change and how can you reframe them?
- What habits can you create to make your life run more smoothly? What tasks do you need to let go of? What can you delegate? What tasks are urgent and important? Where can you store your overflow of good ideas? Where can you keep track of open tasks until they are completed?
- What system can you create to support your calendar and plan your week? When do you do your best work? How can you match your energy to the tasks you most want to accomplish?
- How can you limit distractions in your business?
- How will the tactics you are using get you the results you want? How will your tactics and results work together to support each other?
- What steps can you take to directly generate revenue in your business? Will that action alone generate revenue or is it part of several steps needed to attract clients?
- Where are you headed? How will you get there? How do your personal preferences and true talents influence or support your plan? Do you need to invest in help with creating a clear plan?
- What does your success look like? How does it feel? How many clients are you serving? What results are they achieving? How many hours are

you working? How much money are you attracting? How can you create an image of your success and frequently connect with the feeling it evokes?

You can easily take action in your business, but it's the right action steps that will help you reach your goals. Using the Process of ALLOWING Clarity, connect to the vision of your business success and how it feels. Link the actions you take to the results you want to produce and stay focused on your goals.

If you want more support around exploring and experimenting with this chapter's exercises, schedule a free Clarity Call (amandahyoung.com/free).

Chapter 11 – Allow Growth

"What can I learn from this? What will I do next time I'm in this situation?"
Carol Dweck

Even if you follow every step in the Process of ALLOWING Clarity, along with the success, your business will experience challenges and you'll struggle to find solutions. This is normal and necessary. Obstacles will appear. It's how you choose to greet them that will affect your outcome. If you see obstacles as setbacks or annoyances, they will delay you and be bothersome. If you choose to see obstacles as opportunities for learning valuable life lessons, you can embrace them and show gratitude. Learning to welcome and embrace obstacles is part of the learning process that makes you a better entrepreneur. Allow yourself to have a growth mindset and continue to learn from all of life's experiences.

In this chapter, we'll touch on three ways you can allow growth in your mindset. You can choose to struggle in your business, or you can shift your thinking to allow the answers to come to you. You can choose to worry about money and struggle on your own, or you can allow money to flow in and out of your business as you invest in the help you need to achieve your desired results. You can accept that starting your own business and achieving success as an entrepreneur is hard, or you can choose to believe that it is easy.

Allow the Answers You Need

In the corporate world and business school, we're taught that to achieve our dreams, we need to go out there, take action, and get what we want. Chase your dreams. Climb the corporate ladder to success. All these ideas reinforce the need to work hard to be successful and do so in an active way where you take what you can get. That's how I was formally trained as an entrepreneur. I truly believed with all my heart that if I put enough time, money, and effort into my business, I'd be successful. Although it didn't guarantee happiness, the freedom to spend time with my family, or that the work I did would be any good, I was taught that "hard work pays off."

What I've learned from starting my own business is that the opposite – allowing the answers to come, taking inspired action, and working smarter – is far more accurate. When you allow your business to unfold, design it to support your needs and expose your true talents, you allow your business to become successful in a much easier and gentler way. You don't have to climb a corporate ladder or work hard for your money. You can define your success and work smarter while serving more clients and achieving better results.

When you shift your energy from a place where you need to actively chase your success, to a place where you attract success easily, you'll find yourself choosing to go with the flow instead of forcing results in your business. Instead of attending a networking event and seeking out every person who could potentially support your business, you can make peace with the idea that just by attending the networking event, you'll attract exactly the right people you need to meet. Instead of thinking you need to do more on social media, you can allow the right clients to find you at the locations and events that work best for you. Instead of worrying that you aren't doing enough in your business, or you haven't achieved enough success, you can rest easy knowing that no matter where you are in your process, you are exactly where you need to be.

A wise person once introduced me to an idea that forever changed me: You can choose to swim upstream, against the current, and see where it gets you, but it is far easier, and more fun to swim downstream, with the current, and enjoy the ride. It's your choice.

Reflection questions: Are you swimming upstream or downstream? How can you choose to go with the flow of your business instead of trying to force the results you want?

Allow Money to Flow

Money is a form of energy. It constantly flows in and out of our lives. Sometimes that flow is effortless, other times it can be one-sided. The key is to believe that, as energy, money is something that isn't "spent" but is free-flowing. When you release money, by investing in the results you want, you allow space for more money to appear in its place. You don't have to "kiss your money goodbye." Instead, know that you'll see it again soon. Money comes and goes. When you see it as energy and a way to invest in the results you want in your business and your life, you can see it as a way to allow others to invest in the results they want, through you.

From a Law of Attraction standpoint, if you want others to invest in results through you, you need to invest in the results you want to see in your business through others. You can choose to struggle on your own, or you can invest in the help you need to achieve your desired results.

A wedding photographer client of mine realized she had inadvertently designed a very seasonal business. In her slow months, she wanted to stay busy by attracting a different clientele. We worked together to identify potential markets she could target to keep her studio busy in the off-season. She could have struggled with cash flow and tried the Spaghetti Method of marketing to see what stuck after months of trial and error. But her business was too important to her and she wanted results more quickly, so she took meaningful action. We drafted a plan to expose her to a secondary audience of favorite clients – professionals in need of headshots – and provide a steady stream of income to her business.

Reflection questions: How can you attract money into your business? What do you need to invest in to get the results you want in your business?

Allow Success to be Easy

You can accept that starting your own business and achieving success as an entrepreneur is hard, or you can choose to believe that it is easy. Your business doesn't have to be a constant struggle. It's sure to be challenging along the way, but the more clarity you have around what you want, how you want to feel in your business, and how you want your business to support you, the easier it will be to take deliberate action toward your goals and realize your success.

Using the Process of ALLOWING Clarity, an intuitive client of mine was able to identify her favorite client for the first time after years of struggling in her business. She was able to give her favorite client a name and connect with her on a deeper level to uncover her hopes, dreams, and desires. Then my client knew what services to offer and the results to provide to be of the highest service to her clients.

When you allow clarity into your business, you show success a clear path to your door. Instead of wasting time struggling to make decisions, you'll be able to take deliberate action in your business. Instead of investing money in strategies that fall flat, you'll invest in smart ways that produce results. Instead of being paralyzed by too many choices, you'll know the next steps to take to achieve the results you desire.

Reflection questions: What are you making harder than it needs to be? What can you do to make things easier in your business?

Find Clarity

On your journey to find clarity in your life and your business, know that you are not alone and that it can be a challenging process. This doesn't mean it has to be hopeless, overwhelming, or feel impossible. Finding clarity is about connecting with your true self on a deeper level so you can design your business selfishly. Release the importance you assign to what others think of you and listen to your heart. Identify your favorite clients and offer to lead them through a process that helps them in a valuable way.

Finding clarity means you communicate clearly with your clients and inspire referrals. You notice your own needs and give yourself permission to invest in the support you need to become a successful entrepreneur. You deliberately take imperfect action toward your goals, to create the life of your dreams and a business that you are proud of. You allow your desires to reveal themselves, instead of endlessly trying to chase them down.

Clarity in your business isn't an animal to be hunted, but a unique beauty to be patiently awaited and blissfully observed. Instead of exhausting yourself by swimming upstream, allow yourself to go with the flow. Give yourself permission to trust yourself to create the business you desire with grace and ease. Allow the answers you need to appear, listen to what you hear, and take action in a manner congruent with your purpose and your true reason for being in business.

When you think you are off track and doing everything wrong, take comfort in knowing that you are exactly where you need to be. Take time in your business to reflect on your successes and your failures, then act on what you've learned.

Reflection questions: What did you learn from a recent challenge in your business? What can you do differently in the future? How can you improve?

Summary Checklist

Embrace the obstacles you face in your business and welcome the challenges that arise as opportunities to learn and grow. Then apply what you've learned to achieve your dreams.

- Are you swimming upstream or downstream? How can you choose to go with the flow of your business instead of trying to force the results you want?
- How can you attract money into your business? What do you need to invest in to get the results you want in your business?
- What are you making harder than it needs to be? What can you do to make things easier in your business?
- What did you learn from a recent challenge in your business? What can you do differently in the future? How can you improve?

* * *

My wish for you is that the Process of ALLOWING Clarity helps you work through the questions and challenges you face on your entrepreneurial journey as you design a unique business to achieve your goals. Using this process, I hope you will fast forward through the more challenging parts of entrepreneurship to allow more time for sharing your true talents with your favorite clients and creating waves of positive change in the world.

When you find the clarity you need to move forward in your business, go forth and serve your favorite clients with confidence and courage. Lead them to the solutions they seek and serve them from your highest level. Embrace your victories, large and small, along the way and celebrate your success. And know that help is available whenever you find yourself in need of more clarity in your business.

If you already know you want more guidance on your journey to finding clarity in your business and need expert help to accelerate the process, sign up for a free clarity call at amandahyoung.com/free.

Acknowledgments

My heart is overflowing with gratitude for all the people who have inspired and contributed to this book in so many ways. Big thanks go to coach Angela Lauria, editor Grace Kerina, and the entire team at Difference Press for their amazing support, outstanding coaching, and focused guidance to make this emotionally turbulent process so enjoyable. Thanks to Jeanne Dulaney Andrus for suggesting this process and cheering me on along the way.

Thanks also to Christine Kane, her programs, and her entire team for teaching me the importance of leading your clients. Sara Arey and Elaine Bailey, for coaching me through the fires of entrepreneurship. Leah Jackman-Wheitner for cutting through the crap and holding me accountable to my business. Debby Rauch Lissaur for showing me my strengths at lightning speed. Heather McCutcheon for helping me connect with my intuition and introducing me to Reiki. Krish Surroy for highlighting my feminine power. Christine Sonnen for showing me what's possible and teaching me the world of ThetaHealing. Jodie Harvala for introducing me to my spirit guides.

Thanks to the fiercest chick I know, Kelly Ruta, and her outstanding ability to uncover the deepest parts of my inner self. Darryl Stewart for digging up and ditching my dirt! Jeanine Blackwell for teaching me how to teach others. Jennifer Blumenthal for being an intuitive genius.

Gina Bender for showing me what the cards had in store for my future. Robbin Jorgensen for bringing out the firecracker within me. Lindsey Rainwater for being an outstanding guinea pig. And for the clients I've had the pleasure of serving and learning from as we selfishly designed our businesses.

Thanks to my entire family for their support, patience, and understanding during this delicious journey.

About the Author

Amanda H. Young, MBA, is known for helping visionary entrepreneurs focus on the steps they need to take to design, create, and grow service-based businesses they love. She provides much-needed focus and clarity to business owners who have unique talents to share with the world. By cutting through the clutter and getting to the core of her clients' strengths and capabilities, Amanda aligns the services they provide with the people they are meant to serve and simplifies their message and marketing in a way that attracts clients effortlessly.

After studying business administration, marketing, international business, entrepreneurship, and photojournalism at the University of Iowa, Amanda obtained her Master of Business Administration in Nonprofit Management from the University of Wisconsin–Milwaukee. She has a wide breadth of experience working with solo-entrepreneurs and established business owners in a variety of industries, including real estate, manufacturing, architecture, interior design, structural engineering, event planning, life coaching, photography, education, personal styling, payroll, financial planning, vacation travel, and human resources.

With a keen eye for helping her clients find the clarity and confidence to move forward in their business, Amanda offers easy and creative solutions for entrepreneurs in need of a branding foundation or marketing overhaul, and the next steps to focus their marketing efforts and attract clients.

Amanda lives outside of Chicago and has two magical children. She is a voracious reader and knitter.

Thank You!

For more help finding clarity in your business, take advantage of these opportunities:

Free Companion Workbook

For a step-by-step guide through this process, download the free companion workbook of exercises and questions to help you focus your thoughts, gather your ideas in one place, and design your business to support your needs. The free companion workbook is available at:

amandahyoung.com/companion

Free Clarity Call

If you already know you want more guidance on your journey to finding clarity in your business and need expert help to accelerate the process, sign up for a free clarity call at:

amandahyoung.com/free

Share Your Success

I love to see how the Process of ALLOWING Clarity helps entrepreneurs so please don't hesitate to share your questions, comments, and success stories with me via email at:

amanda@amandahyoung.com

www.ingramcontent.com/pod-product-compliance
Lightning Source LLC
Chambersburg PA
CBHW060023210326
41520CB00009B/976